# Leaning into the Future

# Leaning into the Future

## Building Beyond the Post–Covid-19 New Normal

Vincent F. Cotter

ROWMAN & LITTLEFIELD
*Lanham • Boulder • New York • London*

Published by Rowman & Littlefield
An imprint of The Rowman & Littlefield Publishing Group, Inc.
4501 Forbes Boulevard, Suite 200, Lanham, Maryland 20706
www.rowman.com

86-90 Paul Street, London EC2A 4NE, United Kingdom

Copyright © 2022 by Vincent F. Cotter

*All rights reserved.* No part of this book may be reproduced in any form or by any electronic or mechanical means, including information storage and retrieval systems, without written permission from the publisher, except by a reviewer who may quote passages in a review.

British Library Cataloguing in Publication Information Available

**Library of Congress Cataloging-in-Publication Data**

Names: Cotter, Vincent F., 1950– author.
Title: Leaning into the future: building beyond the post–Covid-19 new normal / Vincent F. Cotter.
Description: Lanham: Rowman & Littlefield, [2022] | Includes bibliographical references. | Summary: "This book converts change theory into proven practice"—Provided by publisher.
Identifiers: LCCN 2021037150 | ISBN 9781475864038 (cloth) | ISBN 9781475864045 (paperback) | ISBN 9781475864052 (epub)
Subjects: LCSH: Education—Aims and objectives. | COVID-19 Pandemic, 2020—Educational change.
Classification: LCC LB41.C828 2022 | DDC 370.11—dc23
LC record available at https://lccn.loc.gov/2021037150

# Contents

| | |
|---|---|
| Foreword | vii |
| Preface | ix |
| Introduction | xiii |
| **PART I: FORWARD LEADERSHIP** | **1** |
| Chapter 1: "Leaning Forward" | 3 |
| Chapter 2: "Leading Forward" | 11 |
| Chapter 3: "Learning Forward" | 17 |
| **PART II: RETROFITTING SCHOOLS FOR THE 21ST CENTURY** | **23** |
| Chapter 4: Reinventing Schools | 25 |
| Chapter 5: Restructuring Schools | 33 |
| **PART III: THE PROCESS OF TRANSFORMATION** | **45** |
| Chapter 6: Transforming the Leadership Team | 47 |
| Chapter 7: A Transformative Model | 55 |
| Chapter 8: Transformational Lessons | 65 |
| Chapter 9: Getting "It" Right | 79 |
| Conclusion | 83 |
| Appendix A: Performance Assessment Instruments | 85 |
| Appendix B: Leadership Training Module | 99 |

Appendix C: Leadership Skills That Ignite Performance 111
Bibliography 117
About the Author 123

# Foreword

I first met Dr. Cotter in 2018 as we discussed his book *Performance Is Key: Connecting the Links to Leadership and Excellence* and the opportunities for how to improve professional learning for administrators. As the state association for administrators at all levels (superintendents through aspiring administrators) with over 5,000 members, we provide a significant amount of professional development.

The Florida Association of School Administrators (FASA) is an organization that has pushed our school leaders to reach higher and anticipate the future. Nearly ten years ago, FASA leaders developed over 200 course collections of digital resources aligned to the Florida Standards that were free for teachers anywhere in the country to use. This was not only "pre-pandemic" but also when most teachers were still not sure how to incorporate digital resources into their classrooms. Publishing those resources back then, I never realized how much they would really be needed when school doors were closed indefinitely.

Dr. Cotter's experience as superintendent and creating lasting change for student performance shines through in his latest work. While he acknowledges that the last year certainly showed areas where education needs to develop, he stresses the need to take what has been learned to lead for the future. He provides a platform for vision and shares how leaders use their skills to turn vision into reality.

It has been a transformational year. By nature, educational leaders rise to the occasion to ensure student achievement is the primary focus. Dr. Cotter addresses how to leverage data and a forward-thinking mind-set to lead relentlessly for success. The funding schools have (and will) received from the federal, state, and local level will only support transformation if we implement new practices that can be sustained. We cannot afford to throw the baby out with the bath water. We must adapt with what we have learned, especially our traditional public schools. This school year brought more school choice than we have ever offered, and it allowed students and parents an opportunity to experience education in different ways. How can we offer differentiated learning and maintain integrity of a high-quality education? If leaders are willing to follow through with Leaning into the Future, we can achieve this goal.

I have spent the last 10 years working with Florida school leaders, I remain in awe of how the best leaders engage in new learning, transform practice, and ensure high expectations for student achievement. I look forward to what comes next.

Michele L. White, CAE<br>
Executive Director of the Florida Association of School Administrators<br>
Certified Association Executive

# Preface

### RETURNING TO NORMALCY: "STASIS" OR CHANGE

After each major crisis, we, as a country, often have retreated within ourselves. We become risk averse and seek out the familiar. We long to return to the safety of previous routines and practices. History has provided many such examples.

After World War I, known as the "War to End All Wars," we developed a policy of isolationism. Consequently, the United States was initially reluctant to enter World War II, but at the war's conclusion the nation emerged as a "super-power." Later, the Korean War and the Vietnam conflict generated a reluctance by leaders to commit American troops around the globe.

Much like military conflicts, social issues, protests, and periods of unrest often generated a desire to "return to simpler times." During the last ten years we have experienced a tumultuous political climate. Ideological swings sent the pendulum of governing in various directions. New mandates and revised policies left schools juggling priorities and programs.

Prior to the pandemic, many schools and school districts struggled to meet state, national, and global performance criteria. Far too many students fell below the minimal proficiency requirements in reading and math. With the closing of schools during the pandemic, the issues surrounding achievement were only exacerbated. Long-standing inequities involving technological hardware, internet capability, and staff expertise only further contributed to the loss of previously acquired learning, as well as the ability to deliver quality programming.

With teachers attempting to deliver instruction either full time through the internet or in a hybrid format, the stress of meeting the needs of all students and their parents exacted a toll. Parents were working from home. School aged children began meeting with their teachers online with some form of teleconferencing in adjoining rooms. The "new normal" began to "wear thin" over time.

Students longed for their classmates and even missed eating in the lunchroom. One superintendent sought to lower the anxiety level by declaring a snow play day even though the students were learning from home. Obviously, everyone longed to return to some form of past normalcy. The nostalgia of familiar routines and practices seemed a lot easier.

**But What Does a Return to Normalcy Mean?**

Prior to the pandemic, there were dynamic forces within the field of education and external forces on the peripheral that were pressuring schools and school districts to reduce the emphasis on standardized testing, norm comparisons, data collection, and standards. Exiting the pandemic these forces intensified efforts as a result of social and emotional issues experienced by students, parents, and teachers. For the moment, many argued that a moratorium on state assessment and accountability was a reasonable concession given the loss of learning experienced by most students.

While the argument to declare a moratorium appears logical and responsible, it is also clear that many issues were exposed by the pandemic that require immediate attention. The loss of any potential student growth prior to the pandemic has yet to be fully documented and understood. Determining how to regain those losses in the compressed window of an academic year is critical. Additionally, structural issues involving technological hardware and access require immediate intervention. Furthermore, curriculum and student engagement issues require intense examination as to how to best meet the needs of students in the 21st century.

Returning to normalcy is not just an adjusted new normal. The new normal should be a launch pad into the future. The pandemic revealed the potential of technology in the delivery of instruction. It expanded the uniqueness of how each student learns. Much like the business world, how we work, how we meet, and how we learn may have changed forever. Reverting totally to traditional instructional delivery models may be a missed opportunity. Change and reform are possible at the same time normalcy is being restored.

The essential ingredient to managing both a return to normalcy and optimizing this moment in time is leadership. Leadership is indeed the glue that brings together the component pieces and binds those pieces together. With the proper skills and techniques, leaders can create outcomes that are greater than the sum of those pieces, even where turmoil and chaos seem to "rule the day." Spontaneity and motivational "sizzle" can inspire for short periods of time, but well-founded strategic planning is built for the long game.

Inspired by the recent pandemic, *Leaning into the Future: Building Beyond the Post–Covid-19 New Normal* examines the issues that remain in the forefront of school leadership. It is human nature to return to a "state of stasis" after a traumatic event. This treatise acknowledges the flaws that were exposed by this recent pandemic crisis and require immediate intervention.

Increasing performance is not a new issue. There are a multitude of reasons why too many schools/districts are grounded in mediocrity, but inherently in each of those reasons is our lack of "will" or a "fear of failure." Now is not the time to moderate expectations but rather to increase them.

At the same time, this book provides a leadership design that encourages the reader to proactively "lean" into the issues without creating undo stress and turmoil that may unravel the reform process. By tackling these issues with a "Forward Leaning Leadership" Design, schools/districts will succeed in improving the performance for "All" students. "Leaning" places the reader in the "administrative chair" and clearly illustrates the challenges with moving a school or district forward toward real improvement while finding a path through the organizational entanglements that often dissuade others.

*Leaning into the Future* demands that we seize the moment by finally addressing the obstacles for success and higher performance before this window of opportunity closes, perhaps for the last time. "Leaning" provides leadership teams with the fundamental skills and processes to retrofit, reinvent, restructure, and transform schools to meet 21st century expectations. Each chapter provides proven research, strategies, techniques, and recommendations along with a problem-solving activity and case studies. Through assessments, frameworks, training modules, professional development activities, and power point slides, leadership teams are prepared to tackle a transformational initiative.

A common phrase used in the Chinese language for centuries and later quoted in a 1963 speech by John F. Kennedy implied that "a rising tide lifts all boats."[1] For the most part this quote was applied to economic policies. Now more than ever there is a direct application to schools and school districts.

In education, the tide for greater performance has reached our shores. Now is the time to respond to the learning crisis proactively and with purpose. Let us plug the holes in our ship with courage and skill so it can set sail toward a future of high performance and excellence. We must give this momentum the necessary "fair winds" to succeed through strategic and synergistic practices that refocus a school or district's return to go beyond normalcy and transform schools to meets 21st-century expectations.

## NOTE

1. John F. Kennedy Quotations. *Economics, Public Papers of Presidents: John F. Kennedy*, 1962, Remarks in Pueblo Colorado following Approval of the Frying-Pan Arkansas Project (336), August 17, 1962, John F. Kennedy Presidential Library and Museum.

# Introduction

Striving for excellence and higher performance has been an elusive goal for school leaders in the United States. Well-intentioned initiatives were started with great promise only to disappear as the result of directional shifts in the political landscape or as the result of a crisis that neutralized its momentum. *A Nation at Risk*,[1] a report by the 1983 U.S. Commission on Excellence in Education, once considered an imperative for educational reform, has long been forgotten. Bold initiatives like the No Child Left Behind Act of 2001[2] and the Race to the Top[3] were political casualties of shifting perspectives.

Ironically, the creation of high performing schools has always been the gold standard. Even those that may have opposed the rigor imposed by "top-down" governmental initiatives recognized the importance of excellence. The difficult ingredient to excellence is devising the route to get there.

Defining the pathway to excellence has always been a contentious process and one that has stimulated great debate. Local control involving content, methodology, and standards created tension between federal, state, and local agencies. The debate on excellence morphed into concerns about accountability, the use of testing, and the delivery of instruction.

The accountability movement, in its purest form, was never intended to extrapolate into massive, standardized testing programs, but was simply designed to determine the extent of student learning and link the growth or deficiencies to areas of the curriculum. In other words, its design was to target problem areas and remediate them. Measurement and data are not effective or an efficient utilization of resources if they are not directly connected to the delivery of instruction.

It should also be recognized that striving for excellence and higher performance was never at the expense of rigor or relevant subject matter. Without the rigor and relevance necessary to create critical thinking skills, higher performance could not be attained. Excellence seeks approaches to motivate and stimulate higher performance, it is never exclusive. It recognizes that it is necessary to stretch one's ability level in order to reach a new level of potential. Excellence and higher performance are only possible through inclusion and equity of opportunity for all.

Interestingly, most stakeholders would not argue with the premise of reaching excellence or higher performing schools, but somehow, the challenge of reaching such a goal was never given priority status. The states rolled out programs that identified failing schools and addressed those failures in a variety of ways but ultimately the net gain of performance remained relatively the same. Educational leaders became creative in vociferously proclaiming excellence even if the data demonstrated otherwise.

Suddenly, in 2020, the pandemic closed schools throughout the country. The virus created a seismic shift in the educational landscape. It disrupted the traditional delivery of instruction but more importantly, it exposed the existing deficiencies in schools and school districts. Like a giant wave that crashed on a beach, the ensuing tide exposed disparities that were embedded in the quagmire of meaningless reform. Internet access, the availability of computer hardware, teacher training, and district ineptness were always there.

These shortcomings, as well as other discrepancies and disconnections, contributed to our underperforming schools. Why were the shortcomings ignored for so long and who was responsible for addressing them? The answer to those questions is one of leadership or the absence of it. Regardless, these issues were now in the open for all to see.

In the aftermath of this disruption to the learning process, some scholars have suggested that this multilayered crisis presented an opportunity to transform the schools. Others have suggested more typical responses to recoup lost learning by extending the school year, implementing summer programs, increasing instructional time, and eliminating holidays. Still others insist on an infusion of funding from federal, state, and local government or reconfiguring funding mechanisms.

Beyond attempting to sort out the challenges created by this crisis and other more residual institutional issues, *Leaning into the Future: Building Beyond the Post–COVID-19 New Normal* focuses on the importance of skilled and knowledgeable leadership. "Leaning" further recognizes that leadership is the key in the unearthing of the issues that will make a real difference in improving student achievement and performance.

Will the trauma of 2020–2021 create a desire to retreat to the confines of the "status quo" or will this "period in time" give rebirth to the models of continuous improvement and high expectations for "All" students? The answer to the question remains unknown and is open-ended. The landscape of education remains an unfinished canvas. What is known is that this canvas will only be painted by leaders who are unrelenting and make achievement their priority.

These leaders are artists with a keen eye on the horizon. They know that schools and school districts must be crafted and molded around expectations and performance. These leaders will have the strategic skills to operate among various constituency groups to create a landscape that is meaningful for all participants. The opportunity to create this portrait is upon us now.

History has demonstrated that ignoring the obvious can have catastrophic consequences. Letting something simmer under the surface could destroy the well-intentioned programs, initiatives, and possibly the very institution that one may be attempting to improve. Understanding the dynamics of change is critical in making real growth and sustainable performance a reality.

*Leaning into the Future* encourages you to become an unrelenting leader that recognizes the challenges of performance but is also cognizant of how to overcome the obstructions surrounding them. You are encouraged to join an elite group of leaders who are willing to finally address the real goal of education, student achievement. Now is the time to end the "theater of reform" and build high-performance outcomes for all students.

## NOTES

1. National Commission on Excellence, *A Nation at Risk: The Imperative for Educational Reform* (Washington, D.C.: U.S. Government Printing Office, 1983), https://eric.ed.gov/?id=ED226006.

2. U.S. Department of Education, "No Child Left Behind" Public Law 107–110, *Elementary and Secondary Education Act 2001* (Washington, D.C.: U.S. Department of Education, 2001), https://www2.ed.gov/nclb/landing.jhtml.

3. U.S. Department of Education, "Race to the Top Executive Summary," *ED Recovery Act: American Recovery and Reinvestment of 2009* (Washington, D.C.: U.S. Department of Education, 2009).

# PART I

# Forward Leadership

To confront a challenge and propose viable solutions so that a school or district can close the achievement gap and substantially increase overall student achievement, a "mind-set" that "leans forward" is essential. If leaders possess the prerequisite "forward-leading" modalities, the organization develops organizational cohesiveness. When its component parts are interconnected and integrated through an instructional leadership plan, a school or district increases its potential to "learn forward."

Chapters 1, 2, and 3 illustrate the skills, strategies, and facilitative ability current leaders must use to reach above and beyond. Recognizing that this moment in history provides leaders with a unique opportunity for reflection and action, these chapters encapsulate a leadership philosophy and its key components that provide the foundation to enable a school or district to catapult from underachieving to high performing.

School leaders who seek to truly lead and embrace a mantra of continuous improvement are provided with not only the theoretical content, but also, and, most importantly, the proven practices. Case studies are referenced to illustrate what is possible.

## Chapter 1

# "Leaning Forward"

### FOUNDATION

Unfortunately, there is a crisis in leadership. It exists at the national, state, and local levels. How else can one explain the consistent stagnation of student achievement scores as reported on the National Assessment of Educational Progress[1] and other reporting instruments. How else can one explain the achievement gaps that exist in the schools for years. How else can one explain the recent failures regarding technology and distance learning during the pandemic?

In acknowledging these deficiencies along with others, governmental and local leaders shifted the explanation of these results as a function of funding formulas, demographics, and other socioeconomic factors. Others have attributed the lack of focus on numerous more pressing diversions and distractions. Besides safety issues, school leaders are besieged with challenges to standards, assessment procedures, disciplinary practices, curriculum content, and the overall social-emotional well-being of students.

Increasing technological demands, legislative reform initiatives, teacher protests involving working conditions, the pandemic, and the social justice movement left those in the field of education overwhelmed and exhausted. Amazingly, these crises dramatically exposed the disconnections that have undermined achievement and the drive toward excellence. Suddenly questions regarding how instruction is delivered, the relevance of what we teach, and how we learn resurfaced exponentially.

The desire to really increase student achievement was always there. It was always disguised in the form of slogans, assessment rallies, or purchased programs, which often resulted in little or no progress. Glossing over student achievement in this manner was an injustice to students, parents, and well-intentioned teachers who were seeking substantive solutions. Unrelenting leadership leans into the achievement issue with objective data, structure, and uncompromising outcomes.

## "LEANING INTO AN ISSUE"

Have you ever noticed that before an athletic competition that the athletes "lean forward"? Whether the event is a sprint or a long-distance competition, the athletes prepare themselves mentally by first envisioning the race and, second, by physically "leaning forward." Swimmers lean forward on the starting platform, track competitors lean off the "starting blocks," and professional baseball players always step into a pitch. Why?

In each case the athlete desires the advantage of a good start, but at the same time it reflects a determination to embrace the challenge ahead. A baseball player is literally synergizing their body's muscles to provide additional momentum and the subsequent strength. Stepping toward the ball provides greater kinetic energy at the point of contact. No less important is the preparation prior to each event.

National leaders like John F. Kennedy, Franklin Delano Roosevelt, and Abraham Lincoln were courageous when confronting such events as the Cuban Missile Crisis, the Recession of 1937, World War II, the Civil War, and slavery. Each leader conducted research, consulted, and leaned into the crisis because failure to do so would have been catastrophic.

The scale of the crisis in a school or district is certainly different, but the instructional components to solve the issue are very much the same. Research, consultation, consensus building, and action are all necessary. Identifying the disconnections and reconnecting the instructional threads are crucial. The missing link is possessing the skill to accurately diagnose and strategically develop a plan.

The current "COVID-slide" and its tangential issues are the equivalent to Russia's launch of *Sputnik*. The Russian launch of a satellite into space was a clear challenge to our government and educational system. It was a time to "step up" or fall behind on the world stage. With school and district education programs interrupted by the pandemic, researchers have projected a significant slide in learning and retention.

The actual effect of the slide has been dramatic. "The School District of Philadelphia reported a 15 percent drop on first grade tests. Camden (NJ) further reported a 30 percent decline in high school mastery of mathematics and language arts while the highly regarded West Chester School District notes a similar decline in kindergarten readiness."[2] The Los Angeles Unified School District indicated the following startling declines:

- More than 13,000 middle and high school students disengaged from learning in 2020.
- Two out of three students fell behind in literacy and math.

- Only 44 percent Black and 43 percent Latino students remain "on-track" for early reading readiness.[3]

Improving our academic performance is therefore a priority because the window of opportunity will close. Acknowledging our failures in a nonjudgmental manner is a beginning to healing and solving the current learning gap in achievement. "Leaning forward" begins with an objective framework of assessment, connectivity of elements, and expectations.

## INFORMATION GATHERING

Consider the introductory lyrics of a 1970s rock opera song "What's the Buzz? Tell Me What's a-Happening."[4] These lyrics appear as relevant as ever. Knowing the internal "vibe" of a school or district is critical. Without having an "ear to the ground," self-imposed pitfalls in the implementation process are inevitable.

In preparing for the achievement challenge, a school leader must recognize the importance of research, analysis, and execution. Most importantly, a leader must understand the uniqueness of each school culture before wading into the "deep water." On the surface, the school or district may appear like any other educational environment.

Beneath the operational surface of each school or district is a unique culture. Regardless of size, location, and resources, there is a subtle or overtly traditional approach to accomplishing its mission. Statements like, "We've always done it this way," or, "That's the way we do it," may reflect operational expediency while ignoring inherent values of the organization. It is therefore not surprising that the unique dynamics, history, and underlying politics can either make or break the desire to move forward toward substantive performance.

Culture is like a virus. It will fight to survive. It will mutate and disguise itself. In schools or school districts, culture is embedded in the organization's practices, policies, and beliefs. Over time, it indoctrinates those within it.

Having been assigned as a teacher and principal in several school districts and later selected as superintendent in another school district, I was amazed at how different culture can impact every decision, discussion, and everyday practice. Culture is the security blanket for maintaining the "status quo," or it can be the most powerful impetus for change.

Understanding the culture is time consuming but necessary. Working in a toxic or an unresponsive culture is frustrating. Molding a culture around achievement, higher performance, and excellence is even harder.

To understand the school/district's culture, a leader must listen, dialogue, and gather information. It is no longer possible to announce that you are the new leader and expect everyone to follow you. Unfortunately, there are "sacred cows" and "lines in the sand" that a leader needs to discover.

Michael Bloomberg expressed the importance of crossing those lines and addressing the existing power structure before a generation of learners are lost.[5] Union leaders vested in keeping power by injecting control over managerial decisions need to reexamine their role considering this generational crisis. Embedded internal procedures and practices that prevent innovation and change require review and revision.

Rest assured that these traditions, practices, and policies are temporary, if you are committed to improvement and implement strategies to circumvent them. Reacting to an existing culture without totally understanding it and how it impacts the organization is a strategic mistake. Internal relationships established over years are difficult to change. Transformation necessitates strategic and synergistic skills.

Having knowledge of internal personal relationships and where those relationships intersect with practice and policy assist in needlessly stepping on a "land mine." These strategic traps come in many forms, both formal and informal. Avoiding these strategic "set ups" requires an understanding of previous decisions and the rationale for those decisions. Making a wrong decision without sufficient background knowledge can taint or even stereotype the leadership team in a way that may take years to undo.

Shifting the culture requires unrelenting leadership. Even so, the emotional wear and tear in attempting to change organizational direction can result in a leader succumbing to the "status quo." Frankly, a path of acquiescence is much easier.

It is less stressful to "go with the flow" and keep everyone happy. Any change in direction will even make some well-intentioned faculty unhappy. Strategic leadership knows how to move change forward without undo turmoil. It recognizes that time is a valuable commodity in the process.

A shift in culture will not happen immediately but gradually. The light at the "intersection of growth" does not automatically change from red to green. It is a much slower process involving "small wins" and victories. Change will be embraced when a consensus built upon a sense of urgency and common purpose becomes the prevailing climate. Building a consensus to undo the ingrained practices of the past involves a degree of risk.

It then comes as no surprise that as the "dashboard lights" of student achievement continue to "blink red," leaders too often choose the path of least resistance as the organization moves forward with no tangible outcome in sight. Content to drift toward the horizon, these leaders are more than willing to keep the "status quo" intact. The engine might be smoking but the illusion of making progress may be good enough.

A better approach is to have leaders pause to examine the engine and determine how to improve performance before taking the next step. Not only do you need to "kick the tires," you need to get under the hood.

## CONNECTIVITY

Each year the *Oxford Dictionary* introduces new words and phrases into its annual publication. If there was a category for nominating a "word of the decade," the term *connectivity* might qualify for consideration. With the infusion of technology into our personal, social, and individual workspaces, connectivity of technology and hardware has become an essential component to the effectiveness and efficiency in our daily lives. Imagine the confusion and frustration if one's computer, printer, and other devices were periodically offline or, for that matter, if the world went offline for even a millisecond.

Likewise, it is somewhat surprising that many schools and districts have a laisses-faire approach to the connectivity that drives the organization. "Leaning" an organization forward toward progress and growth involves connecting its alignment, atmosphere (culture), accountability, and administrative leadership. Gaining insight into the connectivity of those key elements assists the leaders and the team in the identification of systemic issues that are impeding achievement.

Armed with data from such assessment tools as the Schools Systems "Cross Check" (appendix A, A-1, A-2, A-3) and the Hierarchy of School/District Development (appendix A, A-4), leaders can begin building plans to improve performance. From these instruments and other similar diagnostic tools, school and district leaders can objectively determine the misperceptions between various groups like school board members, administrators, teachers, and community members. A matrix and tabulation of results often reveal diverse views on the crucial components that drive the instructional program.

For higher performance and excellence to gain a "strong footing," all constituents groups must interpret and understand the component parts that are required for success. They must build associated instructional plans for execution in the same manner. Consistency of implementation throughout all levels of the organization is an indication of "buy-in." Every aspect of the plan must "fit like a glove" for a school or district to reach its desired outcomes.

## EXPECTATIONS

Creating a "new normal" that lowers standards and expectations is a superhighway to mediocrity. Unfortunately, the new normal is an admission and benign belief that the leadership team, teachers, and students are not capable of meeting the challenge of higher expectations. Nothing could be further from the truth. In part, failing schools suffer from leadership teams that have not found the structure to create excellence.

Expectations are not exclusionary. Instead, high expectations are inclusionary. "Raising everyone up" involves providing skills and a knowledge base to all students. With this base, students will have the opportunity of career choice and the potential economic freedom. With marketable skills and talent, students will walk in the sunlight of a dawning horizon.

Forward leadership focuses on creating a structure of cohesiveness that produces high level performance. The pieces of the achievement puzzle are already on the table waiting for leaders to assemble them. It is possible to fill the voids in the achievement gap through systemic structures (K–12) that are designed to bind the organization together.

Leadership without a framework results in disjointed solutions and haphazard outcomes. Unrelenting leadership is focused and leans into the problem with real solutions that result in higher performance outcomes. When confronted with an issue, it never gives up until the goal is reached.

James Thomas Anthony Valvano, affectionately known as "Jimmy V," was head coach of the North Carolina State basketball team. In 1962, Valvano was diagnosed with metastatic bone cancer. ESPN recognized his achievements at an ESPY program, at which time he delivered a now-famous speech, "Never Give Up."[6] Valvano emotionally stated that "time is precious." He encouraged those in attendance to remember "where you are and where you are going." He further encouraged leaders "to think every day, to have emotion and enthusiasm in what you are doing but never ever give up."

Unrelenting leadership never gives up. It is reflective. It solves problems with tangible solutions that produce higher performance. Structure, standards, expectations, and data are not the problem. Excellence and higher performance are not the problem but rather the solution.

## REFLECTIVE QUESTIONS

- Take a moment to reflect on how you "leaned" into an issue. How did you gather information regarding the problem? How did you identify the underlying contributing factors to the problem and establish expectations in rectifying it?

## SUMMARY

- Several data points indicate that a crisis in leadership has existed for some time.
- The recent pandemic has exposed existing and current deficiencies in education.
- Prioritization of achievement issues has been replaced by distractions and diversions.
- The philosophical underpinnings of "forward leadership" involve leadership "leaning" into issues, gathering information effectively, connecting key organizational elements to optimize outcomes, and having higher expectations for achievement and performance.
- "Leaning forward" is objective and nonjudgmental in remediating school and district deficiencies.
- Structure, standards, expectations, excellence, and higher performance are not the problem in solving declining student achievement.

## RECOMMENDATIONS

- Provide leadership training to team members to "lay the organizational groundwork" for the philosophy and framework associated with forward leadership (appendix B).
- Organize meetings with key internal communicators in ascertaining the strengths and weaknesses of the organization.
- Conduct assessments that measure the perception of vested constituent groups regarding the instructional effectiveness.
- Focus on key organizational elements (alignment, atmosphere [culture], accountability, and leadership) (appendix A, A-1, A-2, A-3).
- Ascertain the perceptions and aspirations of school leaders regarding a school or district's current and projected development (appendix A, A-4)

## PROBLEM SOLVING

A school district with a history of underperformance was in search of a solution for this ongoing problem. Initially, the district invested in professional development programs that were provided by external experts. Since little growth transpired, it supported a "Pay for Performance" plan (merit play), which guaranteed the consternation of the faculty and teacher's union. The issue became the focal point of the district's contract negotiations. As the superintendent of schools, how would you assist in resolving this stalemate? (See chapter 8, case study #3.)

## NOTES

1. National Assessment of Educational Progress, "National Assessment of Educational Progress (NAEP): Nations Report Card," Washington, D.C., last modified 2019, https://nces.ed.gov/nationsreportcard 2019/.

2. Maddle Hanna, Kristen A. Graham, and Melanie Berney, "COVID-19 Has Upended Education: How Will Schools Solve the Learning Loss?" *Philadelphia Inquirer*, April 8, 2021, https://www.inquirer.com/education/a/pennsylvania-education-students-pandemic-learning-loss-20210408.html.

3. Howard Blume, "LAUSD Students Suffered Alarming Harm during Pandemic," *Los Angeles Times*, March 31, 2021, https://www.latimes.com/california/story/2021-03-31/lausd-covid-data-show-alarming-learning-harm-report.

4. Tim Rice and Andrew Lloyd Webber, "Jesus Christ Superstar, What's the Buzz Lyrics," *Metro Lyrics*, https://www.metrolyrics/what-the-buzz-jesus-christ-superstar.html.

5. Bradley Cortright, "Bloomberg Says Teachers Are 'Just Going to Have to Suck It Up' and Have In-Person Classes Amid Pandemic," *Independent Journal Review*, February 3, 2021, https://ijr.com/bloomberg-teachers-suck-it-up-have-in-person-classes/.

6. Geoffrey Clark, "Watch: Jim Valvano Gives Memorable 1993 ESPYs Speech," *USA Today*, December 8, 2020, https://www.fightingirshwire.usatoday2020/12/08.

*Chapter 2*

# "Leading Forward"

## LEADERSHIP MODALITIES

"Forward leadership" recognizes that there is fluidity in the style required to accomplish high-performance outcomes. How one leads at any given moment is the result of a variety of variables. The internal dynamics of the organization may exert relational pressure on the leader at any given point in the improvement process. Successful leaders know how to adjust to any such pressure in a strategic and tactful manner.

Successful leaders use change modalities along a continuum of leadership practices based on the "vibe" and "on-the-ground" feedback. To implement a program or initiative regardless of the level of internal resistance is simply a recipe for disaster. The goal is to skillfully adjust strategy in building consensus so that it appears as a designed part of the process. If done properly, the leader can maneuver around obstacles in a logical and supportive manner. This type of leadership maneuvering is often perceived positively.

While "leading forward" is focused and driven toward higher performance, the leader must never appear insensitive to well-intentioned motives of staff members. Any substantive directional change can risk offending those educators that have previously participated and supported other programs to improve achievement. Key data points should be objectively presented to those staff members as a means of building support. Objective data removes the sharp edges around an initiative when moving groups from a "status quo" position.

Leaders who are successfully "leading forward" often find it necessary to use multiple strategies to accomplish the designated mission. They are always strategic, supportive, and synergistic. When these modalities are implemented simultaneously, leadership becomes "synertegic."

## Chapter 2

## "SYNERTEGIC LEADERSHIP"

"Synertegic" leaders know how to combine the modalities of strategy and synergy.[1] Strategy involves an analysis of a leader's options regarding procedural maneuvering as it relates to policy implementation, planning, and execution. Synergy is the human energy released when building a unified critical mass in the execution of an idea or a plan.

Integral in creating synergy is building consensus. Reaching real synergy can be a tedious and time-consuming process, but it is well worth the investment. It involves listening to individuals and groups, as well as using persuasion techniques as members of the school or district are gradually and subtly moved toward the desired change. The goal is always the universal endorsement of the objective, but adept leaders recognize that a consensus majority is generally more realistic.

A strong emotional quotient that connects higher performance to the individuals who are implementing the objective is the intangible ingredient to success. Simply knowing one's "x's" and "o's" is not enough to build consensus. Having the ability to "sell" the urgency to change based on data alone is insufficient.

Rather, leaders must connect the concept of improvement to a school or district's belief system. The values of the organization are essentially its "North Star" to guide it forward even during moments of confusion and mistrust. Simple pontification or pronouncements "to get it done" is not enough. Instead, leaders must attempt to earnestly listen to opposing perspectives and even to disjointed rationale from those that may be internal disruptors. Leaders do not have to agree with those desiring to stall growth, but adept leaders need to provide resistors with a logical alternative.

A "synertegic" leader understands that substantive growth does not manifest itself overnight. Gradients of momentum are accumulated over time and are only energized when there is a critical mass to sustain the reform or change. Informative coaxing provides time for the leader to build the necessary "ground swell" to reach a "tipping point" for consensual acceptance.

"Synertegic" leaders examine data, the validity of the results, and the accuracy of the data. Decisions regarding the applicability of the data in solving achievement problems are made by astute leaders. This type of leadership uses critical thinking in its analysis as to the effectiveness of current programs and policies. This type of leadership further critiques future programs with a laser focused lens on how any expenditure will improve performance.

No program, practice, or policy is beyond the scope of "synertegic" analysis. Leaders prod, critique, and ask the right questions in drilling down to the bottom line. With a mandate to go beyond the "status quo," a leader explores performance initiatives with flexibility. In attempting to identify which levers of achievement are most effective, the cost of the program is examined in the context of performance. When the confusion created by needless programming is lifted, instructional clarity emerges. Almost immediately as the fog of incongruency dissipates, a unity of purpose drives the organization to new heights.

The "synertegic" process is inclusionary. In committing to the concept of Gestalt,[2] which states that the whole is greater than the sum of its parts, the "synergetic" leader recognizes the importance of teamwork and how supporting those that are working toward the common objective maximizes an outcome. A "synergetic" leader is resourceful in assisting those executing the mission by removing obstacles.

While obstacles come in many forms, "time" is considered the most important. There are only so many hours in a school day. With instructional time in competition with so many operational and mandated programs, teachers are often frustrated as to when they can collaborate to dialogue about improvement. By eliminating the obstacle of time for dialogue and creative planning, a "synertegic" leader demonstrates an understanding of a legitimate problem and designates achievement as a priority. At the same time resistance is lowered and support for change is increased.

When the time issue is addressed, collaboration begins. It will require facilitation and support, but it will empower those involved in the process with the power to create solutions to the dilemma of underachievement. The identification of the issues as well as action plans to address the problem must come from within the school or district.

## "SERVANT LEADERSHIP"

Balancing the modalities of strategy, synergy, and support is the overlay that each "synertegic" leader is a servant leader to the school and district community. In 1970, Robert Greenleaf coined and published the term *servant leader*. In his writings, Greenleaf stated, "It begins with a natural feeling that one wants to serve. Then a conscious choice to aspire and lead. That person is sharply different from one who is leader first, perhaps because of the need to assuage an unusual power drive or to acquire material possession."[3]

The "synertegic" leader embraces the concept of service to school and community. By understanding the importance of student achievement and its exponential impact on the future of a student, the "synertegic" leader is willing to commit to all organizational elements to improve performance. Embracing an agenda for improvement involves some level of risk in terms of program failure and career advancement. Conversely, to the extent that there is little or no pressure for change, the risk of maintaining the "status quo" is minimal.

In many schools and districts, the key to succeeding as a leader is keeping everyone happy. Too often leaders are allowed or even directed to maintain the status quo. The mantra of "not rocking the boat" maintains low expectations and eventually permeates throughout the entire school or district. By not "setting the bar high" or providing both the teachers and students with the skills to get there, a leader is essentially not serving anyone.

Not critiquing the effectiveness of how a school or district progresses in reference to normative standards is essentially benign neglect. To "glad hand" and congratulate those that have contributed to the failure of students, even if those efforts were well-intentioned, is disingenuous to those that they are entrusted as a leader. To proclaim that a school or district is the best or exemplary when the data clearly shows otherwise can only be described as malpractice.

Confronting the achievement issue, intervening and constructively developing an effective plan for improvement is the ultimate responsibility of the servant leader. Such a leader places the student and the community first. Instruction becomes the priority. The shift in priorities relegates noninstructional activities, while important to the overall morale of the school, to become secondary when competing for finite resources.

A "forward-thinking" leader with a "synertegic" approach is clearly focused on improving the lives of the students through improved performance. One's ego is secondary to the success of the students, the teachers delivering the program and to the community that they serve. Service defines this leader in his/her commitment to excellence and performance for all students.

## REFLECTIVE QUESTIONS

- What are the necessary steps in developing a consensus?
- As a leader, how would you facilitate the steps to building consensus?
- What leadership modalities did you apply moving a faculty toward consensus?

## SUMMARY

- "Leading forward" is always strategic, synergistic, and supportive.
- In implementing a "leading forward" mind-set, a leader has the latitude to adjust approaches based on a school or district's internal dynamics.

- Data and objective analysis are fundamental in lowering internal resistance to change.
- "Synertegic" leaders know how to combine the modalities of strategy and synergy.
- A strong emotional quotient is necessary as part of building a sense of urgency.
- Substantive growth is not automatic.
- "Synergetic" analysis results in a determination of the effectiveness of programs, policies, and practices that impact instruction.
- The "synertegic" process is inclusionary, requires teamwork, and removes obstacles to learning.

## RECOMMENDATIONS

- Review appendix C to explore leadership skills.
- Elicit samples of synergy in your organization.
- Examine the elements of synergy.
- Identify blocks of time for teacher collaboration.

## PROBLEM SOLVING

The school district has gone to great lengths to change its culture and improve student achievement. Building goals connected to district goals are now formulated by a School Improvement Team. Principals select a building team to develop annual goals. The team is composed of teacher leaders at the school.

The principal communicated to the central office his/her concern that the plan which was developed by the team is not reflective of the data or specific areas in need of improvement to generate higher student performance. The team in developing the plan also delegated responsibility for its implementation to the central office. The principal has met with his/her school improvement team several times to change the plan, but they are adamant that the plan more than adequately meets the district's vision. As the leader of this district, how do you assist in the resolution of this issue? (See chapter 7, stage 3, "School and District Planning.")

## NOTES

1. Vincent F. Cotter, *Igniting School Performance: A Pathway from Academic Paralysis to Excellence* (Lanham, MD: Rowman & Littlefield, 2019), 13.

2. Merriam Webster, "Gestalt," https://www.meriam-webster.com/dictionary/gestalt.

3. Robert Greenleaf Center for Servant Leadership, "Start Here: What Is Servant Leadership?" accessed April 2017, https://www.greenleaf.org/what-is-servant-leadership/.

*Chapter 3*

# "Learning Forward"

## COHESIVENESS

Student achievement has been an issue for some time. With the pandemic exacerbating the achievement gap, Dr. Robert Avvossa indicated, "Addressing learning and the achievement gap as the #1 priority of superintendents."[1] Other identified areas of concern include teacher morale and cultivating a culture of care; special education services; fostering social emotional learning and student wellness; and funding during COVID-19 and beyond.

While these identified areas are not new to practitioners, the lack of longitudinal progress regarding student achievement and the issues that support it, directly or indirectly, remains surprising. Despite well-intentioned efforts, billions in annual expenditures, and legislative initiatives, consistent excellence and higher performance elude far too many schools. While the pandemic and other future crises may highlight specific issues, it is only through the incorporation of systemic instructional planning and cultural cohesiveness that will solve them. Specifically, cohesiveness which makes achievement a priority eliminates mission confusion and disconnectedness.

We are what we value. Schools and districts are very much the same. Take a moment to review what they value. School and district websites revel in its activities, athletic accomplishments, music videos, and artwork. Extracurricular events dominate their public relations pages while a relatively small amount of content is dedicated to academics, in terms of course offerings, programs, and so on. An analysis of several inner-city high schools highlighted an array of art, inspirational music and slogans.

Efforts to motivate and inspire are lauded but "miss the mark." They are an attempt to solve a problem without substance and structure. Many of these programs include speakers, a video, a message, or even programs that are well received by the staff and community. Unfortunately, the outcomes are not long lasting and are not interconnected to the overarching goal of improved student performance.

"Learning forward" goes beyond the superficial in organizing a cohesiveness that will produce results. In overcoming such major issues as underachievement, the learning gap, and equity, leaders must structure a cohesive system that links the component parts of achievement in a manner that produces results. It is through this linkage and connectivity that the potential of students emerges.

## SYSTEMIC COHESION

Systemic cohesion links all the facets of a school or district to its core values and mission. For optimum student achievement to occur, the key performance factor elements of systemic alignment, atmosphere (culture), accountability, and leadership are linked to its desired outcomes. When there is a strong interrelationship and connectivity between these items and a district's values, academic growth becomes a reality. The strength of the relationship is reflected in the results.

When there is a high degree of connectivity there is a greater level of effectiveness, which results in higher student performance. Where there is a lower degree of connectivity, the number of disconnections is higher, and effectiveness decreases. A "learning forward" school or district embraces connectivity and cohesion because it defines its vision, goals, practices, processes and strategies in the language of achievement. Not only do action plans define the improvement process but they assign accountability for them.

Systemic cohesion requires alignment strategies that are synergistic and strategic in creating consensus, developing goals, devising action plans, researching policies, establishing best practices, and developing measurable indicators and outcomes. Cohesion involves reflection and analysis, and it is data driven. In essence, when the district and school are aligned to reach the same goals, there is systemic cohesion.

## INSTRUCTIONAL COHESION

Instructional alignment is much more than traditional strategic planning. At its core are the fundamental designs that drive instruction. When a school or district determines that achievement is its priority, all instructional and operational components reflect that decision. Funding, resource allocation, personnel deployment, and program approvals are impacted.

By simply asking how a budget will impact student achievement, another layer of scrutiny is added to the process. Examining resource allocation based on performance and how to disperse personnel to underperforming schools is another dimension of the instructional alignment process. It can be a painstaking process, but it is essential when conducting administrative due diligence.

Administrative academic "due diligence" forces the integration of performance criteria into programs, curriculum, evaluation, and supervision. This additional type of scrutiny generates cohesiveness because the organization begins to function with common purpose. Simple ratification of programs without understanding the scope and impact that a program has on achievement is negligent. Prior to advancing any aspect of an initiative for implementation or board approval, administrators must ask such probing questions as the following:

- How does this program or initiative advance student achievement?
- What data or evidence demonstrates that this program will achieve its goal?
- How will its outcomes be measured?
- Who is ultimately responsible for its success or failure?
- Is there any duplication of programming?
- How does it fit into our current efforts?

No one likes to answer questions. It is not always considered supportive, but at the same time no one should assume a defensive posture because at the heart of every question and decision process is the achievement and interest of the students. Every inquiry should be framed around the following beliefs:

- All children can learn and achieve.
- Students come first.
- Failure is not an option.
- Higher performance is our goal.
- Nothing can take the place of quality instruction.
- Investing in the internal capacity of the organization to increase performance is funding well spent.
- Consistency in the teaching learning process occurs when there is accountability.

## CULTURAL COHESION

In the movie *Goodfellas*,[2] actor Ray Liotta tells his brother to keep stirring the (tomato) sauce. For the sauce to reach its maximum flavor, all the ingredients must be thoroughly blended. Schools and districts are not much different. Leaders must blend all the components in an integrated but aligned manner so that the organization can reach its full potential.

Cohesiveness of culture is a function of its personnel understanding the school or district's systemic alignment in accordance with its values and beliefs associated with higher performance. How an organization communicates and executes its alignment is related to the level of understanding and support for its alignment. Tangentially related is the consistency to which the plan for improvement is executed.

Culture is overtly defined by its instructional attitude toward the alignment and performance plans. It is either perceived as positive or negative based on the degree in which instructional solutions are genuinely sought and the extent that the curriculum reflects rigor, relevance, engagement methodology, and overall quality. A work ethic that collaborates and perseveres in delivering a results-based program is representative of attributes that are found in instructionally strong cultures.

Leadership is crucial in nurturing a cohesive climate. Leaders with the intuitive ability of knowing when to facilitate, when to provide support or technical expertise, and when to assert themselves tend to develop trust among staff members. A collaborative environment of shared responsibility, transparency, and fairness increases morale.

> "Shifting the mind-set" toward performance and achievement requires a focus on team, collaboration, and integrated beliefs. Recent studies found that a "teacher's own mind-set, whether he or she believes students' intelligence and skills aren't inherent and fixed, is a strong predictor of student engagement and academic performance, as well as the severity of race-linked achievement gaps between students."[3] Believing in the mission of improving the achievement levels of students can make a major difference. "For example, teachers who help students to learn alternative strategies had students who were 3.5 percentage points more likely to have a growth mind-set."[4]

Synergy occurs when everyone focuses on the mission. Staff members are adapting instruction, providing support, collaborating and accepting constructive feedback. Internal accountability is accepted when there are transparent targets, shared responsibility in meeting them, and fairness in the evaluation process.

When an organization builds internal capacity through skill acquisition and professional development, the culture endorses collaborative accountability. It is no longer feared due to inclusion in the decision-making process. School improvement teams assist in maintaining instructional focus while encouraging experimentation and action research.

## REFLECTIVE QUESTIONS

- Where is cohesion evident in your school or district?
- How can a leader build stronger systemic, instructional, or cultural cohesion?

## SUMMARY

- The achievement gap was identified as a national priority issue by school superintendents.
- We are what we value.
- Cohesiveness is the glue that produces consistency and results.
- Systemic cohesion's key factors include alignment, atmosphere (culture), accountability, and leadership.
- The degree of connectivity is tangential to the level of performance.
- Instructional alignment is not strategic planning.
- Administrative due diligence is required to determine the extent of program integration.
- At the heart of every probing question is the achievement and best interests of the students.
- All inquiry should be framed around the school and district's beliefs.
- Cultural cohesion is related to the level of understanding and support regarding district alignment.
- "Shifting the mind-set" toward performance and achievement issues requires a focus on team, collaboration, and integrated beliefs.

## RECOMMENDATIONS

- Review appendix C, slides 7 to 12.
- Identify your school/district priorities.
- Locate evidence regarding what your school or district values and where that evidence is found.
- Determine your school/district's level of connectivity and rate on a scale of 1 to 10, with 10 as the highest ranking. If necessary, how can you improve?
- Describe the administrative academic "due diligence" in your school/district's approval process.
- Rate your school or district's culture of achievement (on a scale of 1 to 10). Where is improvement necessary?

## PROBLEM SOLVING

In a district of 5,000 students and 7 schools, most of the schools are making significant progress in meeting their targeted academic goals. Two of the seven schools appear to be struggling. One is marginal in meeting both reading and math proficiency standards. The remaining school clearly has not been able to "move the needle" on student achievement and is listed as "Not Meeting" proficiency standards in reading and math by the state. If this trend continues one or both schools may be listed as "turnaround" schools and eventually subject to takeover or closure. How do you as the district leader rectify this issue? (Review chapter 4, "Reinventing Schools.")

## NOTES

1. Robert Avossa, "Looking to June: Top Five Learning Priorities," *Learning Counsel*, 2020, https://www.thelearningcounsel.com/article/looking-to-june-top-five-learning-priorities.

2. Martin Scorese, dir., *Goodfellas* (Los Angles, CA: Warner Brothers, 1990).

3. Sarah D. Sparks, "Growth Mind-set Linked to Higher Test Scores, Student Well-Being in Global Study," *Education Week*, April 21, 2021, p. 4.

4. Sparks, "Growth Mind-set Linked to Higher Test Scores," p. 4.

# PART II

# Retrofitting Schools for the 21st Century

The wide-ranging impact of technological and social issues requires reexamination by our schools and school districts. How schools plan to deliver instruction and respond to the social and emotional pressures exerted on them will shape school quality long into the future. The outcomes resulting from this introspection and subsequent planning from it will either drive schools toward higher performance or recenter them around mediocrity.

Chapter 4 examines the historical evolution of schools as they adjusted to societal and economic shifts and provides examples of how schools can reimagine and repurpose their mission to meet the demands of the 21st century. Chapter 5 further highlights the importance of addressing equity, technological challenges, social-emotional issues, physical infrastructure, civic responsibility, and health policies as they restructure for the future.

*Chapter 4*

# Reinventing Schools

## THE EVOLUTIONARY NATURE OF SCHOOLS

To paraphrase Charles Darwin, a species survives by how it responds to change.[1] Unlike a species, an organization makes a conscious decision as to whether it should adjust or maintain the "status quo." Both a species and an organization evolve due to environmental pressures. Those pressures change its behavior, and those adaptations, likely impact its relevancy in the future.

Schools and districts can choose to change, but ultimately their failure to respond to external feedback can have negative consequences. Ignoring data and feedback can result in enrollment shifts that threaten its viability. Schools with extensive histories of serving generations are often shuttered in urban centers due to decreasing enrollment or the lack of a vision that meets the needs of those that they serve.

COVID-19 accelerated a decade-long decline in urban enrollment as families opted for such alternatives as homeschooling, choosing to delay the start of kindergarten, or accessing virtual learning.[2] The implication of those familial decisions may have lasting effects on schools because they could potentially impact future decisions about the delivery of teaching and learning. Attendance declines in high-poverty school districts result in per pupil expenditure reductions.

Initially, schools were designed to reflect the values and traditions of an agrarian society. Schools were small and town oriented. School schedules were adjusted to meet the demand of the planting and harvesting cycles. Much later, the Industrial Revolution and urbanization restructured school design. Schools became much larger to accommodate the increasing population of the nation. Rather than one room schools structured to meet the instruction of many age groups, urbanized schools had several teachers organized by grade level.

Globalization, with its reliance on the internet and technology, again shifted the educational landscape. The focus on high-level "STEM" related skills began to raise issues regarding quality, rigor, and relevance. Teaching and learning appeared to develop a greater reliance on the integration of technology into everyday instruction.

The pandemic and the associated economic crisis stimulated a plethora of pressures from various constituencies. It is unprecedented that such simultaneous issues as equity, technological access, social-emotional sensitivity, and curriculum relevance have been the focus of improvement. The question of where to start looms even greater in the ever-increasing shadow of the growing achievement gap.

For schools to continually evolve, they must embrace the concept of continuous improvement and higher performance for *all* children. The continuous improvement research of Larry Lezotte[3] and others has long believed that schools must go beyond the facade of reform and embrace continuous improvement in every facet of the organization. A starting point begins with a recognition of its deficiencies and a belief that a school or district has the internal capacity to remediate them.

Evolving schools must demonstrate the courage and "will" to change. They are innovative in philosophy, practice, content, and technique. They are open to experiment and think "out of the box." They are responsive to internal and external pressure but recognize that criteria involving excellence and standards are fundamental for sustainable reform.

The leadership team in an evolving school is committed to internal innovation that seeks alternative and potentially nontraditional solutions. These solutions are not purchased through an instructional materials company but rather are developed internally. Evolving schools control their own destiny. Leaders in these schools realize that you can either wait for the future to arrive or you can shape it now. They prefer to reimagine their schools now.

## REIMAGING OUTCOMES

Issues surrounding excellence, performance and quality have plagued schools for decades. As far back as 1970, the book *Savage Inequities*[4] by Jonathan Kozol highlighted the plight of those attending urban schools. Now imagine inserting a virus that closed schools for more than a year into some of those same falling schools. The projected performance outcomes are predictably obvious.

Recent work by researchers at NWEA, a nonprofit provider of student assessment, estimated that "students would complete the year (2020) with only 40 to 60 percent of the learning gains that they'd typically see in a school year."[5] Other research groups reported a smaller loss that amounted to the equivalent of three months. Additionally, since subject matter involves the scaffolding of content from a foundational base, specific learning gaps were bound to develop.

In a separate analysis of 800,000 students, researchers at Brown and Harvard universities found that through late April 2021, student progress in math decreased by about half in classrooms located in low-income zip codes.[6] According to McKinsey and Company, black and Hispanic students could experience an equivalent of 10 months of learning loss and the average student could fall behind by 7 months.[7] Fareed Zakaria, a CNN analyst, reported similar projections.[8]

Closing of the schools due to the pandemic was further compounded by existing issues of inequity of online access, technical difficulties with distance learning, and the overall lack of personalization that remote learning typically produces. Faced with inequities within and across school districts, teachers reported administrative directives to "scale back" expectations. Some districts reduced instructional time, while others were instructed "not to teach new material" because "there were concerns about the huge discrepancy in the parent's ability to manage home teaching."[9]

Some districts feared an increasing number of student failures. Fairfax County, Virginia, reported an 83 percent increase in academic failures during the pandemic.[10] Similar data was reported in the Independent School District of Houston and in St. Paul and Minneapolis, where 40 percent of high school students reported as receiving failing grades.[11] Fairfax County School District data indicated there was a correlation between socioeconomic status, student temperament, learning disabilities, and home stability to successful online learning.[12]

Other schools prohibited the failing of students. In March 2021, it was reported that a "Baltimore City high school promoted a student to twelfth grade despite failing three major subjects. In fact, the transcript for this student placed him in the middle of his class with a grade point average (GPA) of .013."[13]

A few districts opted for a continuation of standards by announcing that there is "no such thing as a COVID-19 pass."[14] Still others reported a high degree of teacher stress and declining morale. Student depression soared to record highs.

Considering the previously illustrated learning deficiencies that were exacerbated by the virus, school leaders have proposed traditional solutions, for example, the following:

- Identifying opportunities to recover instructional time from the existing school day.
- Finding time and resources for high-impact support.

- Moving students into grade-level-appropriate content in the new year rather than repeating material from the end of the prior grade.
- Ensuring teachers have information about what students know and can do.
- Facilitating communication across grade levels.[15]

Starting the school year earlier, creating mini-courses or devising a semester course format may assist in efforts to address the COVID learning slide and to prevent learning gaps. While education experts suggested that recouping lost learning may involve acceleration academies (aka summer school), tutoring, and more equitable schools, Mark Schneider, a researcher at the Department of Education's Institute of Educational Sciences, recommends that the "United States spend more investment on research and evaluation of what really works in education."[16] Much like DARPA in the Defense Department, Schneider has proposed spending $3 million for transformative research in the educational sciences.

Even though the "sound bites" regarding increased funding and research resonate through legislatures and other political entities as reasonable solutions, practitioners must search for solutions to the learning issues exacerbated by COVID-19 that are realistic and expedient. Matching existing resources to current funding levels may generate more "out-of-the-box" thinking and creativity involving the reallocation of staffing, regrouping of students, and scheduling. Learning issues which are more systemic may require a more transformational approach.

While the situation may appear bleak, this crisis does provide an opportunity for schools and districts to reimagine themselves. School leaders and teachers should feel empowered to reinvent the schools. With its shortcomings exposed, leaders can not only develop interventions to recover lost learning, but also devise long-term solutions.

The pandemic crisis has provided clarity to the importance of in-person instruction. Technology is an asset, but without personalization online instruction begins to produce diminishing returns. The grind of daily "zoom" instruction was evident in the faces of those receiving it. Technology is simply a mechanism to support direct instruction and not replace it.

The pandemic has illustrated many issues that require improvement. The potential for evolutionary change and innovation is real. Now is the time to finally get it done. Imagine a higher performing school where the following takes place:

- Ninety percent of all students are proficient in reading and mathematics.
- Student achievement continues to statistically improve in each school year.
- Achievement gaps are eliminated for all demographic and learning groups.

- Honors and advanced placement courses are a prominent part of the curriculum.
- Student assignments involve critical thinking activities.
- Flexibility exists in the delivery of instruction.
- Creativity is encouraged.
- Experimentation and action research are the norm.
- "Out-of-the-box" solutions are sought.
- Interdisciplinary instruction and project learning are embedded in the curriculum.
- Classroom instruction is engaging and participatory.
- Leadership is collaborative and inclusive.
- Teachers are empowered.
- Parental involvement is positive and constructive.
- Improvement is continuous and never done.
- Going "above and beyond" is not just a slogan.[17]

Reinvention is indeed possible when you are willing to jettison the ineffective practices of the past and unconditionally accept the premise that performance and excellence are evolutionary when schools confront the present status and plan to effectively meet the challenges of the future.

## REFLECTIVE QUESTIONS

- Is your school or school district evolving or maintaining the status quo?
- Have you as a leader committed to creating a school that reflects excellence and higher performance?

## SUMMARY

- Adaptation likely impacts the future relevancy of an organization.
- Ignoring data and feedback can have devastating consequences.
- Schools evolve in response to societal and economic pressure.
- Reform is paramount in the shadow of an ever-increasing achievement gap.
- Evolving schools are not constrained by traditional solutions.
- A crisis can sharpen the leadership's focus on shortcomings and solutions.

## RECOMMENDATIONS

- Determine the developmental level in the context of school improvement (see Hierarchy of School Development, appendix A-4).
- Create a "triage" list of failing or nonproficient students with designed and individualized remediation for each.
- Formulate a list of potential solutions for students or groups in the achievement gap.
- Reconfigure resources to adapt to potential enrollment shifts or lack of funding, or to target academically challenged students.

## PROBLEM SOLVING

The high school course offerings were limited. It was unclear as to why the school never expanded its offerings. It appeared that the leadership lacked an aspirational vision or a belief that the students were not capable of successfully completing more challenging work. Did the leadership think that the obstacles were too great to overcome? As the district's instructional leader, how do you assist this principal to overcome his or her hesitancy to risk such a change. (Hint: See chapter 8, case study #4.)

## NOTES

1. Charles Darwin, *On the Origin of Species: By Means of Natural Selection; the Preservation of Favoured Races in the Struggle for Life* (London: John Murray, 1859).

2. Victoria Lee, Emily Gutierrez, and Kristin Blagg, "Declining School Enrollment Spells Trouble for Education Funding," *Urban Wire*, October 6, 2020, pp. 1–4.

3. Lawrence W. Lezotte and Barbara C. Jacoby, *Sustainable School Reform: The District Context for School Improvement* (Okemos, MI: Effective School Products, 1991).

4. Jonathan Kozol, *Savage Inequities* (New York: Harper Perennial, 1991).

5. Heather C. Hill and Susanna Loeb, "Teachers Will Need to Work Together to Uncover Missed Learning," *Education Week*, May 27, 2020, https://www.edweek.org/ew/articles/2020/05/28.

6. Dana Goldstein, "Research Shows Students Falling Months behind during Virus," *New York Times*, June 5, 2020.

7. Goldstein, "Research Shows Students Falling Months behind during Virus."

8. Freed Zakaria, "Last Look: Schools in the Age of COVID-19," *CNN*, April 4, 2021, https://www.cnn.com/videos/tv/2021/04/04/exp-gps-0404-last-look-on-schools.cnn.

9. Catherine Gerwertz, "Instruction during COVID-19: Less Learning Time Drives Fears of Academic Erosion," *Education Week*, May 28, 2020, https://www.edweek.org/ew/articles/2020/05/27/instruction-during-covid-19-less-learning-time-drives.html.

10. Hannah Natanson, "Failing Grade Spike in Virginia's Largest School System as Online Learning Gap Merges Nationwide," *Washington Post*, November 24, 2020.

11. Natanson, "Failing Grade Spike in Virginia's Largest School System."

12. Natanson, "Failing Grade Spike in Virginia's Largest School System."

13. Tom Tillison, "Report: Baltimore H.S. Senior Passes Just 3 Classes in 4 Years, Still Near Top of His Class," *BPR: Business and Politics*, March 5, 2021, https://www.bizacreview.com/2021/03/05/report-baltimore-hs-senior-passes-just-3-classes-in-4yrs-still-near-top-half-of-his-class.

14. Gerwertz, "Instruction during COVID-19," p. 4.

15. Hill and Loeb, "Teachers Will Need to Work Together to Uncover Missed Learning," pp. 4–5.

16. Anna Kamenetz, "Keep Schools Open All Summer, and Other Bold Ideas to Help Kids Catch Up," *NPR Education*, February 8, 2021, p. 2.

17. Vincent F. Cotter and Robert D. Hassler, *Performance Is Key: Connecting the Links to Leadership and Excellence* (Lanham, MD: Rowman & Littlefield, 2019).

*Chapter 5*

# Restructuring Schools

**DELIVERING INSTRUCTION**

In many ways, the pandemic crisis was a teacher's worst nightmare. Much like a student being disruptive in class, for which there is no relief, sending them to the principal's office might momentarily quell the outburst, but it may not immediately resolve the underlying issues that the behavior might have exposed.

For years, school districts developed elaborate safety plans to protect students from intruders or those planning some form of violence. School districts also assisted local county health and emergency departments with their planning by providing bed space and access to their facilities for shelter or to assist in the distribution of food. Some districts planned evacuations and conducted drills in the aftermath of Three Mile Island, but few planned for an event such as the current pandemic.

Ordered to remain at home except for essential services, school districts, for the most part, found themselves in "uncharted waters" without immediate and practical options to keep the instructional program alive. A few districts with significant technical capability were able to restore some semblance of instruction, but even weeks into the crisis many school districts struggled to find viable and instructionally sustainable solutions.

To be fair, the pandemic was an unprecedented historical event; however, the technology to keep the instructional program going had been available for some time. It was just not considered a necessity or a priority. Prior to the pandemic, some progressive districts saw the power of technology by providing its grade-level and subject-based curriculum on their websites, along with recommended activities. These districts required that teachers post their lesson plans and provided parents access to their grade books to assist and support both students and parents. Obviously, during the pandemic, this level of technical investment paid dividends.

During this crisis, the value of technology has been clearly demonstrated, but it has also illustrated the inequity that continues to exist in far too many school districts. Larger urban and rural districts were reluctant to distribute computers or tablets due to insufficient numbers of those resources. State regulations further prohibited the distribution unless fairness and equity could be guaranteed. Some technology and cable companies "stepped up" by providing free "laptop" computers or access to the internet, but too often, insufficient district infrastructure and nonexistent advance planning for use presented obstacles.

Amazingly, in a country of wealth, where millions are glued to "hand-held" devices daily, millions of Americans lacked basic broadband or simply could not afford it.[1] This digital disparity raised further questions as to whether the U.S. government and telecom industry should have done more previously to solve the divide. With such an existing divide, equity and fairness are not possible.

At the same time, shuttered schools raised issues regarding deficiencies associated with instructional time, curriculum relevance, and instructional substance. Unanswered questions of how to meet the required hours and number of school days in a manner that is authentic and meaningful remain unanswered. Simply ending a school year without defined criteria for promotion in 2020 communicated conflicting messages regarding rigor, relevance, and instructional time. With closures continuing through 2021, questions of recouping lost student learning intensified.

Throughout the country, states struggled with solutions to balance state requirements with uniqueness of local control. Moving forward with the future solutions to such dilemmas, restrictions and regulations should yield to flexibility and creativity so that schools and districts are not unnecessarily restrained. Freeing schools and districts from restrictive mandates also provides them with more options for resource deployment.

The pandemic crisis has provided a forum in which to begin a dialogue to resolve the technological divide between the "haves" and the "have-nots." In addition, the crisis has also created opportunities to discuss long-standing instructional issues regarding how education is delivered and approaches that cross over the boundaries of time and space. Flexibility regarding time and space has the potential to unleash creativity that results in a myriad of sustainable solutions capable of reinventing the delivery of curriculum and instruction.

We already knew the important role that schools provide with instruction and mental health programs, and as a hub of community activity. We know how important it is to educate *all* children. We also know the key components that need to be "tweaked" for schools and districts to perform at their highest level.

## EQUITY

All children have a right to maximize their learning potential, but results from the National Assessment of Educational Progress (NAEP) and other standardized assessments have illustrated that this goal has been elusive for many students.[2] To confront the issue of underperforming schools, the Race to the Top invested $4.35 billion under the American Recovery and Reinvestment Act of 2009 (ARRA).[3] The act defined state success factors in developing a coherent plan of reform, but these factors varied widely.

In 2009, the city of Boston went as far as defining fundamental assumptions to provide quality programming.[4] These six assumptions included the following:

- Effective instruction
- Student work and data
- Professional development
- Shared leadership
- Families and community
- Adequacy of resources

Other components embedded in these assumptions included the alignment of policies and plans, diverse cultural leadership, expectations, assessment, and accountability for performance.

Even as Boston outperformed its urban counterparts in 2013,[5] it was implied that although they were among the best urban districts in the country, they were still unable to "compete with many suburban districts around the nation."[6] The apparent disconnect between underachieving and higher performance involves the maintaining of rigorous standards, as well as a curriculum that delivers quality. While a report from the Chief of State School Officers on the "Indicators of Science and Mathematics Education" (2007) indicates an "increase in algebra 2 and chemistry enrollment nationwide, major questions remain regarding our ability to compete at the global level."[7] Schools remain ranked 31 out of 79 in math literacy.[8] Research has further suggested that the achievement disconnect is the result of engagement techniques.

Dr. Jo Boaler, mathematics professor at Stanford University, suggests the elimination of the "geometry sandwich," which involves the teaching of algebra 1 (9th grade), geometry (10th grade), and algebra 2 (11th grade) in a sequence.[9] Rather, Boaler recommends teaching all three together in a form that integrates statistics, data science, and computer analysis, coupled with coding. Other researchers have suggested greater opportunities for problem solving to stimulate creativity.

Another form of disconnection includes the level of complexity involving student assignments. Rather than simplistic fact-finding, learning activities should be structured in a manner that requires critical thinking. These activities can take place in the early grade levels through interpretation of data, graphs, and writing. The incorporation of problem-solving, written skills, and the ability to communicate differentiates the complexity of instruction by the shear nature of the assignments. Through this process students learn the importance of fact versus opinion. Other options for increased rigor include interdisciplinary education.

Interdisciplinary programming has been the missing link in the development of high-quality instruction. It remains an untapped avenue for the integration of skills. It does provide situational learning through case studies and analysis. When implemented with a defined structure that incorporates rigor and relevancy, it may address several of the issues surrounding time, standards, and mandates. It requires collaboration across disciplines and flexibility with student grouping. Project learning is a form of interdisciplinary instruction that is promising.

Project learning, in its most simplistic form, involves a research topic. The topic is screened by teachers or a committee for its appropriateness and rigor. Ideally, the approved project or action research integrates the fundamentals of mathematics, science, English, and social studies, along with the arts in solving a specific problem. Many such projects incorporate a strong STEM component.

The project can follow many avenues to reach its intended goal, which is the demonstration of sufficient knowledge in key subject areas. Such an exercise should also demonstrate a sufficient commitment of time and subject treatment. This interdisciplinary approach might allow schools and districts to meet various standards and requirements in an authentic and substantive manner.

Selecting the effective teaching materials has also been found to increase performance.[10] As a cost-effective measure for improving achievement, one study involving five states found that "effective teaching materials were attributed to 0.1 standard deviation increase in math learning among fourth and fifth graders. The increase equated to the difference between having a novice teacher versus an experienced teacher."[11]

The options are virtually limitless when seeking approaches to leveling the "playing field" as it relates to quality. STEM, robotics, and academic courses can combine a dimension of learning with unique skills in a personalized environment. Action Research "opens the door" to "out of the box" thinking in attempting to solve a specific problem. The net result in implementing alternative approaches is increased creativity.

Change is not the hard part. Knowing what to do and how to do it is "where the rubber meets the road."

## SOCIAL EMOTIONAL SENSITIVITY

In creating higher-performing schools, there is recognition of the importance of educating the whole student. The use of standards and achievement data requires an analysis of the social and emotional factors that may impact student performance. Each student must feel accepted and comfortable in one's instructional environment to maintain the focus on learning.

Recently, educators have rededicated efforts to understand the full impact of social and emotional issues on the learning process. The Collaborative for Academic, Social, and Emotional Learning (CASEL) defined the scope for supporting children and adults in terms of "understanding and managing emotions, impulse control, setting and achieving goals, feeling positive, and showing empathy in establishing and maintaining positive relationships which assist in making responsible decisions."[12] The importance of Social and Emotional Learning (SEL) programming cannot be understated given the number of student suicides during the pandemic. Nevada's Clark County School District alone reported 19 suicides in a district of 326,000 students.[13]

In Pennsylvania, Act 18 was signed into law on June 28, 2019, amending Act 44.[14] The new provisions established requirements related to safety and security supported the creation of a "Trauma-Informed Approach," which is now part of the Pennsylvania Public School Code. The act further stipulated the need for training by board members and employees.

In the integration of such legislative mandates as Act 18, CASEL recommends an analysis of five competencies:

- Self-awareness: Identifying emotions, maintaining accurate self-perception, recognizing strengths, and exercising self-confidence and self-efficacy.
- Responsible decision-making: Identifying problems, analyzing situations, solving problems, evaluating, reflecting, and exercising ethical responsibility.
- Relationship skills: Communicating, engaging socially, and using teamwork.
- Social awareness: Taking perspective, exercising empathy, having an appreciation of diversity, and showing respect for others.
- Self-Management: Controlling impulses, managing stress, exercising self-discipline, setting goals, and having good organizational skills.[15]

Schools that invested in social emotional learning saw increases in student achievement. Everett Public Schools (Washington) saw graduation rates increase from 53.4 percent to 94 percent in a four-year period by instituting a SEL Multitiered System of Support.[16] Oakland Unified (California) had similar results. Through a five-year strategic plan that made SEL a priority, Oakland shifted its culture by making adults accountable for the students' social emotional skills.[17] By addressing the human dimension of education, the SEL skills appear to be longer lasting and useful. While early in its efforts, Oakland Unified believes that the program will improve student performance.

In business, such companies as Blue Cross Blue Shield, Delta, and others have suggested that schools help students to develop resiliency, adaptability, and empathy.[18] Furthermore, it states that digitization and automation increases the demand for technological skills, as well as social emotional skills. Agility, flexibility, resilience, teamwork, collaboration, and the ability to learn were emphasized by Michael Fischer of Sysco Management.[19]

Each of the recommended CASEL competencies is part of a program design for tolerance and understanding. By providing strategies for resiliency students will have a "toolbox" of life skills for handling stress, trauma, and intolerance. Well-adjusted students result in higher performing students.

## PHYSICAL ENVIRONMENT

Schools and school districts have dedicated large amounts of time and funding to "hardening" physical infrastructure to prevent violence from internal and external intrusions. The COVID-19 pandemic also highlighted a school or district's vulnerability to a viral infection. While this unseen enemy had devastating consequences, several aspects of it may have been mitigated through a structural assessment of a facility's HVAC system.

Scientific studies of the deadly COVID-19 virus demonstrated the importance of air circulation. Proximity to an infected individual in a room with poor air circulation was a primary cause of its spread. The introduction of external fresh air and proper HEPA filtering of the air were shown to reduce the spread of airborne microbials.

Prior to this unprecedented crisis, HVAC systems and overall air circulation received little scrutiny. When there was a visual identification of surface mold, schools and school districts conducted air sampling to determine the presence of toxic mold spores. Given that mold spores can cause allergic reactions, including headaches and nausea, the importance of this issue should not be understated. In some cases, the teacher unions and parents forced the closure of buildings until remediation took place. In Pennsylvania, several schools were closed until their HVAC systems and duct work were replaced.[20]

"Significant questions remain regarding the effectiveness and potential impacts on human health"[21] involving the equipment schools are buying to improve air circulation. Current filtration systems that include filters to remove microbials when combined with proven, research-based HVAC devices have the potential of reducing infection. New school designs and renovations should include windows that open to further improve natural ventilation. If schools and school districts regard the physical safety of students and staff as their highest priority, the physical health of students and teaching staff must be added to the list.

## ARCHITECTURE FOR CIVIC INVOLVEMENT

The pandemic and other past crises have demonstrated that solutions are found only when the facts are discussed in a transparent manner. With difficult issues confronting the schools and districts, conversations can be emotional, but it is only through the presentation of irrefutable facts that answers are found. Beyond formal board meetings, school boards should provide ample opportunity for discussion and discovery. Committee and subcommittees are appropriate areas for problem solving but should not be highjacked for political convenience or for manipulative purposes. The leadership of the organization, along with its governing body, as its primary responsibility, must maintain integrity in the process by representing all students and all facets of the community.

Our founding fathers recognized the importance of aspirations by stating, "What we are ought to be rather than what we are."[22] By ensuring that the "machinery of the system works,"[23] stakeholders can collaboratively create an equitable future for all students. The coronavirus pandemic reminded our country that the "public good" involves health, education, infrastructure, and public safety.[24]

Our civic infrastructure supports the activities and interactions through which people gain the motivational and practical capabilities needed to develop a sense of purpose. Fostering our common purpose in the 21st century will require strengthening the existing civic infrastructure that has the capacity to unify disparate segments in our society. The civic process must remain inclusive, fair, and not subject to manipulation by those with an agenda that does not support the common purpose or beliefs of the school system.

The schools and district must further instill in its student body respect for the institutions that are working on their behalf and provide opportunities for involvement at early education levels. We must reinforce the belief that we are "all in this together."

## STUDENT HEALTH POLICY

Neill S. Alexander, founder of the progressive Summerhill School in England who advocated for personal freedom and progressive action, coined the phrase "Freedom not license."[25] In this controversial book for its time, Alexander discusses the balance between freedom and license, which constitutes trespassing on the rights of others. While this treatise is more than 50 years old, the term has even greater applicability now than it did decades ago.

Most recently, COVID-19 has refocused a discussion regarding the government's role in protecting the health, safety, and welfare of the general public in respect to civil liberty, individual rights, and the extent of parental decisions regarding child vaccinations. For years, state departments of health and education, as well as legislative bodies, struggled with finding the balance in protecting a parent's right to make decisions for their child and protecting the health of the general population.

State agencies have sought to limit parental rights when those rights trespass on the rights of the general population that the government is expected to protect. Compounding the issue is the relegation of such decisions to the individual states as determined by the 10th Amendment on matters related to education. In fact, the Centers for Disease Control (CDC) indicates that state laws establish vaccination requirements and any associated exemptions. Each state has established protocols for admission to public school that comply with federal "free and appropriate" education laws (FAPE).

Most states require children who are age four and who are entering kindergarten, prekindergarten, or government day care to have proof of vaccination or evidence of a booster dose for polio, measles, chickenpox, diphtheria, tetanus, and pertussis. After a measles and whooping cough outbreak several years ago, several states tightened the admission requirements. Massachusetts later mandated a flu vaccine for all students.

Since the COVID-19 virus is more contagious than the flu and can spread beyond state boundaries, there may be an argument for a federal mandate to include the coronavirus vaccine as a childhood vaccination. At minimum, states should reexamine existing student health policies. Certainly, any such review should consider those with legitimate religious, ideological, and philosophical objections to childhood vaccinations. Striking the right balance involves providing those with objections with opportunities through virtual and remote learning or home schooling as a means of meeting state educational requirements and federal mandates for a "free and appropriate" education.

## REFLECTIVE QUESTION

- To what extent has your school or district restructured the delivery of instruction to accommodate for issues involving technological advances, equity, social-emotional sensitivity, and health/safety?

## SUMMARY

- The pandemic highlighted issues in the delivery of instruction.
- Proactive schools and districts regularly update their technology infrastructure.
- Equity gaps in technology, content, rigor, and relevancy exist in the nation's schools with a greater frequency than previously reported.
- Interdisciplinary instruction is an untapped instructional methodology that could open avenues for increased rigor and creativity.
- Students must feel comfortable and safe to maintain a focus on learning.
- Creating environmentally sound and healthy environments must be a priority for schools and districts.

## RECOMMENDATIONS

- Conduct an audit of schools and district technology infrastructure.
- Conduct a curriculum audit of school and district offerings to align with those of high performing schools and districts.
- Review all policies and practices to eliminate any obstacles to an equitable delivery of instruction.
- Implement an advanced placement program and honors option for all courses.
- Examine the incorporation of STEM content into the curriculum.
- Formulate a committee to identify areas in which Interdisciplinary Instruction is compatible.
- Examine all classroom assignments and activities for the incorporation of critical thinking.
- Create a social and emotional program (see https://www.casel.org).
- Evaluate all current health protocols and procedures.
- Assign a liaison to the county health department.

- Maintain and/or replace aging HVAC systems and duct work to create greater air flow and quality.

## PROBLEM SOLVING

The school committed to completing an accreditation process every 10 years. Even though the process was voluntary, it provided the school and the district with an opportunity to reflect on the organization. For the most part, the accreditation process of the past involved an examination of the curriculum, student clubs and activities, facility, the quality of the staff, funding, and programs. Quality was measured by numerical counts of the library collections, websites, courses, advanced degrees of staff members, and so forth.

Based on the process, the school was considered excellent on the surface. Unfortunately, comparative standardized measures placed student achievement in the lower half of county schools. The school was clearly underperforming. As the school's leader, where do you begin with the improvement process and the expectation that the school participate in accreditation? How do you transform instruction and learning in the school? (See chapter 8, case study #1.)

## NOTES

1. Tony Room, "It Shouldn't Take a Pandemic: Coronavirus Exposes Internet Inequity among U.S. Students as Schools Close Their Doors," *Washington Post*, March 16, 2020, https://www.washingtonpost.com/technology/2020/03/16/schools-internet-inequality-coronavirus/.

2. National Assessment of Educational Progress, "National Assessment of Educational Progress (NAEP): Nations Report Card," Washington, D.C., last modified 2019, https://nces.ed.gov/nationsreportcard2019/.

3. U.S. Department of Education, *Race to the Top: Game-Changing Reforms, ED Recovery Act: American Recovery and Reinvestment Act of 2009* (Washington, D.C.: U.S. Department of Education, 2009), https://www.ed.gov/open/plan/race-to-top-game-changing-reforms.

4. Boston Public Schools, "Whole Improvement: Six Essentials," *Internet Archive*, 2009, https://www.archive.org/details/publicscho04bost.

5. Boston Public Schools, "Update on Eliminating the Achievement Gap," presentation to School Committee, *Boston Public Schools*, June 18, 2014, https://www.bostonpublicschools.org/cms/lib07

6. Boston Public Schools, "Boston Students again Outperform Urban Peers on Nation's Report Card," *Boston Public Schools*,

December 2013, https://www.bostonpublicschools.org/site/default. aspx?PageTyp...=o47e6be3-6d87-4130-8424-d8e4e9ed6c2a&FlexDataID=3158.

7. Rolf Blank, Doreen Langesen, and Adam Peterman, "State Indicators of Science and Mathematics Education 2007," Council of Chief State School Officers, 2007, pp. 3–4.

8. Erin Richards, "Math Scores Stink in America: Other Countries Teach It Differently and See Higher Achievement," *USA Today*, February 28, 2020, https://www.usatoday.com/story/news/education/2020.

9. Richards, "Math Scores Stink in America."

10. David Steiner, "Curriculum Research: What We Know and Where We Need to Go," *Standard Work*, 2017, https://standardwork.org/wp-content/uploads/2017/03/sw-curriculum-research-report-fnl.pdf.

11. Thomas Kane et al., "Teaching Higher: Educators' Perspective on Common Core Implementation," *Harvard University Center for Policy Research*, 2016, https://cepr.harvard.edu/files/teaching-higher-report.pdf.

12. "What Is Social and Emotional Learning?" *Collaborative for Academic, Social, and Emotional Learning*, https://casel.org/what-is-sel/.

13. Elizabeth Stuart and Leah Asmelash, "A rise in student suicides has pushed the 5th largest school district to speed up a return to in-person learning," January 26, 2021, https://www.cnn.com/us/clark-county-school-district-covid-suicide-trnd/index.html.

14. Pennsylvania Department of Education, "Act 18 of 2019 (SB 144)," June 28, 2019, retrieved at https://www.education.pa.gov/Schools/safeschools/laws/Pages/Act 44.aspx#:~:text=Act%201820%202019%20revi.

15. "What Is Social Emotional Learning?" *Collaborative for Academic, Social, and Emotional Learning*, https://casel.org/faq/#:~:text=SEL%20is%20the%20process%20through,and%20make%20responsible%20and%20caring.

16. Committee for Children 2012–2021, "Moving from All Students to Each Student," *Second Step*, https://secondstep.org/success-stories/everett.

17. Vicki Zakrzewski, "A New Model of School Reform," *Greater Good Science Center-Berkeley*, May 21, 2014, https://greatergoodberkeley.edu/article/item/a-model-of-school-reform.

18. Mark Lieberman, "Top U.S. Companies: These Are the Skills Students Need in a Post-Pandemic World," *Education Week*, March 2, 2021, https://wwwedweek.org/technology/top-u-s-companies-these-are-the.-skills-students-need-in-a-post-pandemic-world.

19. Lieberman, "Top U.S. Companies."

20. Laurie Mason Schroeder, "Another School Closed for Mold," *Allentown Morning Call*, September 9, 2018, https://www.mcall.com/news/breaking/mc-nws-perkiomen-schools-closed-mold-20180909-story.html.

21. Heidi Przybyla, "Federal Officials Seek Better Rules about Schools' Indoor Quality," *NBC* News, May 20, 2021, https://apple.news/A2-CTgeULSpu9xRnLBNE0KW.

22. Thomas E. Ricks, *First Principles* (New York: HarperCollins, 2020), 132.

23. Ricks, *First Principles*, 286.

24. Ricks, *First Principles*, 287.

25. A. S. Neill, *Freedom Not License* (New York: Hart Publishing, 1966).

# PART III

# The Process of Transformation

The process of changing a school or district's practices from those that are traditional or even transitional requires a model that adheres to the organization's transformational beliefs. The goal of transformation is to deliver outcomes that will move the school or district from the "status quo" to one that reflects higher performance.

Chapter 6 recognizes the role of leadership in the transformational process particularly in motivating staff members to embrace the proposed changes. Chapter 7 provides a process to meet the challenges of the transformational process. Chapter 8 provides specific case studies that illustrate the various paths that schools and districts followed toward reform and transformation. Chapter 9 identifies fundamental principles of reform for substantive change. The conclusion aligns the rationale for change and why it is important that we act now.

*Chapter 6*

# Transforming the Leadership Team

### "YOU ARE WHAT YOU VALUE"

Business and industry leaders have long known that performance and productivity are related to the organization's ability to adapt to its environment. Most companies are "customer-centric," but those that are transformational are innovative and "forward-thinking." They can redefine "what they are" and "how they do it." The *Harvard Business Review* analyzed 57 transformational companies based on three metrics: growth, adaptation, and performance.[1] Most consumers are not surprised that Amazon, Netflix, Priceline, Apple, and Aetna are considered the most progressive.[2]

Amazon recognizes that its success is tied to its leadership principles, which are engrained in their culture.[3] These principles are as follows:

- Customer obsession: Start with the customer and work backward to accommodate their needs.
- Ownership: Act on behalf of the entire company and never say "that's not my job."
- Invent and simplify: Be externally aware and look for new ideas from everywhere.
- Right, a lot: Exercise strong judgment and have good instincts.
- Learn and be curious: Always try to improve.
- Hire and develop the best: Raise the performance bar with every hire and promotion.
- Insist on the highest standards: Drive teams to deliver high-quality products, services, and processes.
- Think big: Create and communicate a bold direction that inspires results.
- Bias for action: Calculated "risk taking" is encouraged.
- Frugality: Accomplish more with less. Constraints breed resourcefulness, self-sufficiency, and innovation.

- Earn trust: Listen attentively, speak candidly, and treat others respectfully. Leaders are self-critical and benchmark themselves and their teams against the best.
- Dive deep: Audit frequently, examine metrics, and analyze when there are disconnections in the data.
- Have a backbone: Disagree and commit—have a conviction and be tenacious. Do not compromise for the sake of social cohesion.
- Deliver results: Focus on the key inputs and deliver them.

Adam Bryant, founder of the "The Times Corner Office," indicated that the "most effective leaders need to be able to recruit well, train and motivate, and provide constructive feedback. They need to be able to teach and, more importantly, learn from others."[4] Much like the Amazonian leaders, school administrators seeking higher performance insist on excellence, standards, rigor, relevance, and continuous improvement. These school leaders know the importance of outcomes. They also know how to deliver them.

Known for excellence in educating low-income minority students, the KIPP (Knowledge in Power Program) Public Schools have similar values to those schools seeking higher performance and excellent outcomes. KIPP defines its "commitment to excellence" as a "sustained pursuit, not an end point." KIPP asserts that "excellence is often the 1/12 between good and great."[5] They believe that they can strive for excellence and attain it in all things.

## TRANSFORMATIONAL PRACTICES

Transformational schools aim to change policies and practices to obtain higher-performance outcomes. These schools disrupt the "status quo" and begin to focus on altering every aspect of an organization that impacts instruction. The QED Foundation highlights 23 indicators that are significant in transitioning a school from a traditional position to a transformational organization.[6] The QED Transformational Chart[7] is as follows (see table 6.1):

QED's transformational list is clearly aspirational and extremely aggressive. Given the situational nature of leadership, practitioners might consider using the criteria and projected practices as possibilities for growth. Using the foundation's chart as an informal organizational audit, leaders may begin a dialogue with the leadership team in the evaluation of its own instructional aspirations as a school or district. Implementing every facet of the QED chart is a challenge even for the most progressive and higher performing districts. Every listed transformational item is not necessarily a fit for each school or district.

**Table 6.1 The QED Transformational Chart**

| Criteria | Traditional | Transitional | Transformational |
|---|---|---|---|
| Success | Variable standards | Variable expectations | Consistency |
| Student progress | Text-driven seat time | Standards-based | Proficiency-based |
| Learning pathways | Tracking | Heterogeneous groups | Open access |
| Learning | Scope and sequence | Tasks and projects | Competency-based |
| Learner motivation | Meeting requirements | Interest driven | Curiosity and wonder |
| Personalization | Group instruction | Differentiation | Negotiated plans |
| Learning support | Remediation | Intervention for gaps | Acceleration |
| Responsibility | Student | Teacher | Learning team |
| Learner voice | Parent/teacher | Parent/teacher/student | Student-led |
| Behavior management | Rules | Behavior training | Fostering respect |
| Feedback | Correction | Reflection | Discussion |
| Assessment | of learning | of and for learning | of, for, and as learning |
| Grading | Letter grades/GPA | No zero grading | Proficiency reporting |
| Culture | Based on authority | Based on defined roles | Relationship-oriented |
| Investment in learning | Teacher/student | Teacher/student/family | Community |
| Context for learning | School hours | Extended hours | Any time/everywhere |
| Professional development | Recertification | Learning communities | Community inquiry |
| Learning impact | School relevance | Community relevance | Global relevance |
| Leadership | Seniority | Designated individuals | Everyone responsible |
| Civic mission | Follow and abide | Participate and vote | Engage publicly |

## "SHIFTING THE FOCUS OF LEADERSHIP"

In molding a school or district team, the leader must articulate a philosophical framework based on which the organization will operate. Although building a team with a mind-set for growth takes time, its impact is potentially long-lasting. With the team embracing the leader's philosophy for reform, the challenge associated with groups who initially oppose any change is potentially diminished.

T. J. Sergiovanni suggested that leaders focus on several areas when transforming a team.[8] Specifically, he considered the following aspects of leadership as a beginning point in transforming a team:

- Technical: Sound management of resources.
- Human: Establishment of social and interpersonal bonds.
- Educational: Expert knowledge on educational matters.
- Symbolic: Role modeling and behavior.
- Cultural: Values, beliefs, and cultural identity of the school.

For organizational members to follow a plan, leaders must provide a "vision and communicate that they will embark on a voyage that is going to be useful to them."[9] In other words, the plan will benefit all that participate. When the criteria and principles for transformation are defined, a leader must mold the team in a manner that reflects them. The transformational leadership team must embrace the identified principles with a confidence and belief that upon implementation, a school or district will transition from underperformance or mediocrity to excellence. As leaders overtly model actions through practices that are transformational, faculty members will be more inclined to follow the leadership team. Ambiguity and indecisiveness are not characteristic of these teams.

Instilling confidence requires a reexamination of the leadership team's management style. Through a series of workshops or summer retreat, the team can take a "deep dive" into its vision, beliefs, and mission. School district policies and programs can be analyzed through a "lens" of school district outcomes.

These outcomes for higher performance must address the issues involving the delivery of instruction in an equitable manner along with other problems highlighted by the pandemic. Sensitivity regarding social emotional concerns, environmental infrastructure, and civic involvement may require that the team shift from traditional approaches in rectifying these long-standing problems.

The leadership team can further probe organizational culture by examining its shared values, positive mind-set, collaboration, and openness to change. By reviewing its decision making and problem-solving processes, the team may gain insight into the extent of stakeholder engagement. In allocating time for leadership team building, the groundwork for a creativity, problem-solving, and leadership autonomy is established.

For the most part, superintendents inherit their leadership team. They were active practitioners prior to the appointment of the new leader. Based on the new leader's approach to increasing student performance, existing team members undergo a personal decision as to whether they possess the ability or "will" to effectively perform in the newly designed system. Administrative defections, transfers, and departures are not unusual in the initial stages of change.

Understanding the importance of teamwork and having a commitment to do it are two different propositions. Simply going through the traditional motions of leadership will not suffice. Even in the early stages of transitioning the team, a leader may have to intervene and counsel those that are not embracing the program.

Through exercises that examine a leader's vision, modeling practices, empathy, and inclusionary practices, some team members recognize that the expectations are too great. They realize that they are not "cut out" to lead a transformational program. It requires total commitment because any uncertainty is clearly interpreted by faculty and staff as an opportunity to resist it.

Transformational leadership requires a unified team. These leaders are "willing and able" to confront the disconnections that are obstacles to success. They are willing to honestly "self-critique," read the "tea leaves," and change direction. Indicators and data drive the organization forward. Both the integrity of the leaders and the plans help to build consensus among reluctant followers. Again, these leaders are true to the organizational vision and do not compromise for the sake of social cohesion.

## REFLECTIVE QUESTIONS

- To what extent is your school or district traditional, transitional, or transformational?
- To what degree has your leadership team received extensive professional development in developing a philosophical framework that encourages leaders to move the school or district toward higher performance?

## SUMMARY

- Schools and districts must adapt the culture to an environment that values productivity and performance in order to increase performance and outcomes.
- Higher-performing schools commit to excellence as a sustained pursuit, not an end point.
- Situational factors can dictate the extent of change.
- Leadership teams require molding to reach a transformational level.
- Leaders are willing to submit to self-examination.

- Indicators and data dictate changes to pathways to reach designated outcomes.

## RECOMMENDATIONS

- Review leadership activities in appendix B, "Leadership Training Module."
- Structure a workshop or retreat to review the school or district's leadership philosophy.
- Conduct an audit of the school or district's use of transformational criteria (see the QED Transformational Chart, table 6.1).
- Examine beliefs from business and industry as a reflection to improve school or district performance.

## PROBLEM SOLVING

The central office was organized in a traditional manner. Central office departments included Finance, Personnel, Curriculum and Instruction, Pupil Personnel, Facilities, and Technology. Beyond curriculum supervisors, very few central personnel interacted directly with building personnel. Most central office administrators were focused on compliance matters, including, but not limited to, fiscal accountability or state reporting mandates. There was little or no connectivity to instructional program outcomes. How do you rectify this issue? (See chapter 8, case study #5.)

## NOTES

1. Scott Anthony and Evan I. Schwartz, "What the Best Transformation Leaders Do," *Harvard Business Review*, May 8, 2017, https://hbr.org/2017/05/what-the-best-transformational-leaders-do.
2. Anthony and Schwartz, "What the Best Transformation Leaders Do."
3. Peter Economy, "These 14 Amazon Leadership Principles Can Lead You and Your Business to Remarkable Success," *Inc.*, November 8, 2019, https://www.inc.com/peter-economy/the-14-amazon-leadership-principles-that-can-lead-you-and-your-business-to-remarkable-success.html.
4. Adam Bryant, "Leadership: Building the Skill Set," *New York Times*, 2020, p. 8.
5. "Our Core Values," *KIPP: NYC Public Schools*, https://www.kippnyc.org/about/kipps-core-values/.
6. "Transformational Change Model," *QED Foundation*, June 2012, https://www.qedfoundation.org/transformational-change-model-2/.
7. "Transformational Change Model."

8. Matthew Lynch, "Becoming a Transformational School," *Edvocate*, January 6, 2015, https://www.theedvocate.org/becoming-a-transformational-school-leader.

9. John Dickerson, interviewing David Rubenstein, "How to Lead: Wisdom from the World's Greatest CEO's, Founders, and Game Changers," *CBS News*, September 6, 2020, https://cbsnews.com/news/fulltranscript-of-face-the-nation-september-6-2020/.

*Chapter 7*

# A Transformative Model

## STAGE 1: UNDERSTANDING THE CONCEPTS AND BUILDING BLOCKS FOR SUCCESS

### Organizational Dynamics

Ideas, theories of reform, or frameworks that design outcomes for improved performance rarely are endorsed immediately. Of paramount concern for leaders is how the staff might react to something new. How will a change in the "status quo" impact employee morale? Answering these questions and preparing strategies to avert internal turmoil are crucial prior to any successful launch of an initiative.

Synertegic leaders understand an organization's dynamics before advancing a reform. First, the leadership team must be prepositioned with a thorough understanding of the process and its rationale. These leaders are then strategically prepared to maintain the organization's focus because they are knowledgeable in how to "handle" diversionary and derailing tactics. *It is only when there is an understanding of the process and the possession of facilitatory skills that motivate change that the leadership team is ready to proceed.*

From the outset, school leaders must identify power brokers at each organizational level (i.e., school board, building, parent, community, etc.) and attempt to understand "what really matters" to them. It can be time consuming and frustrating. Reading between the lines and comforting egos require patience.

Power brokers will seek inclusion, particularly if recognition and appreciation are gained through participation. It becomes difficult to oppose an idea when you are part of framing it. If you can educate, motivate, and inspire the power brokers while on the "ground floor" of the initiative, the "ride to the top" is so much smoother.

If you cannot get participants to take the "express elevator" to the top floor in their understanding of how the initiative will benefit them, you will have to "grind it out" one yard at a time. With this scenario the success stories that are incrementally derived from successful implementation will slowly "turn the tide." It is at this critical juncture in the process that the leadership team must remain optimistic in the face of resistance. This cycle, which requires the continual validation of the initiative for its merit, will eventually give way to establishing a consensus.

Much like Malcolm Gladwell's narrative about the resurgence of Airwalk shoes (Hush Puppies) into the fabric of "hipster" fashion, "an idea must reach a 'tipping point' for acceptance to occur."[1] The "law of the few" reiterates the position that a few disproportionately influential people can cause a social epidemic.[2] Similarly in schools, having the endorsement of unofficial power brokers can assist in alleviating fears regarding the proposed changes. In many cases, it has been demonstrated that as few as 20 percent of a group can significantly impact the thinking of the whole.[3] If the constituency groups are nurtured by listening to their issues and accommodating them where necessary, acceptance will take place and spread like "wildfire."

> "Synertegic" leaders recognize that change is gradual. It requires a steadfast determination that the performance outcomes are possible. Change is certainly not for the "faint of heart." Forward leadership continually strives for commitment through collaboration. Without it, it still forges ahead by seeking alternative pathways to reach the "tipping point."

## THE TEACHING AND LEARNING PROCESS

The superintendent and the entire leadership team should be perceived as experts in the area of teaching and learning. When leading a program to reform a school or district, it is no longer sufficient to delegate this critical responsibility for growth to another member of the team, particularly when it is deemed a priority. All leadership team members share in the instructional improvement process.

In the post–COVID-19 era, the ability to close the achievement gap for all students will be dependent on the training provided to the entire supervisory and support team. The mandate that every school strive to attain a higher level of performance as an educational priority has lingered too long on an ever growing list of issues that are competing for finite resources. It requires a team's undivided and continuous focus, particularly now that such issues as equity, social-emotional sensitivity, technology, and critical thinking have been universally identified as 21st-century indicators of successful schools and school districts. Allowing other issues to garner more attention than student achievement will only relegate the schools to years of continuous underperformance.

An immediate step to reverse underperformance is to "raise the bar" involving student expectations. The students are capable of writing at every grade level and in every content course on a regular basis. With the proliferation of technology, every student in every class is capable of research, comparative data analysis and analytical writing.

Rather than the rote repetition of facts, writing should involve the interpretation of the data. Demonstrations of learning become the norm when critical thinking is emphasized. Creativity and problem solving are offshoots of this type of writing and thinking. At the same time, we begin to build citizens who formulate logical thoughts based on fact and provide them with a forum to express them.

## FOUNDATIONAL ELEMENTS OF PERFORMANCE

Organizations thrive when elements that generate performance are linked together. As previously mentioned, the connectivity between the elements of alignment, attitude/atmosphere, accountability, and leadership determines the extent of the organization's successes or failures. This linkage can determine the following:

- The degree to which its beliefs, vision, goals are aligned with its curriculum, methodology, and system of evaluation
- The degree to which the culture embraces the organization's agenda
- The level of responsibility that is shared
- The degree to which outcomes are met

It is the responsibility of the leadership team to facilitate the building of a framework around these critical elements. Consistency is only possible when the disconnections between these elements are eliminated. The current gap exacerbated by the pandemic will only widen unless the action designed to eliminate the gap is tied directly to these elements.

Leaders need to begin to think in terms of the interrelationships between these items versus solutions that are one dimensional. Issues like equity, curriculum relevance, and rigor are broader in scope. These issues are often situationally unique and require individualized solutions.

## STAGE 2: IDENTIFYING AND ASSESSING THE FOUNDATION

### Comprehensive Auditing

Objectively assessing the current status of a school or district prior to implementing a plan for increasing academic performance is critical in ascertaining accurate data for the decision-makers. Facts and research are necessary to chart a direction for remedying deficiencies, identifying instructional disconnections, recognizing ineffective practices, and eliminating obstructive systemic policies. Without this information, a school or district is "flying blindly."

The process of assessment begins with several internal audits. The leadership can determine the invasiveness of each audit. Building support for these audits through guaranteed anonymity assists in reducing defensiveness and helps to generate responses that may be more genuine. The analysis of an instrument's internal validity and overall reliability is helpful. Explaining the rationale and the design of the assessment is valuable in gaining support for it. If perceived as constructive and contributing to the reform efforts, rather than being punitive in some way, participants are more inclined to support the time and effort dedicated to it by the administration.

Whatever the audit results reveal, it is encouraged that the raw data be verified through group meetings and discussions. This type of clarification process is helpful in summarizing trends and eliminating misperceptions. This process of verification adds additional detail to the identified disconnection or issue.

Recommendations that are often listed as immediate, short range, or long range include specific items for action. These recommendations are reviewed with the leadership team prior to organizational dissemination. Often, these recommendations are initially perceived as overwhelming since they are a break from the "status quo" and are transitional or transformational. To reduce anxiety associated with the changes, leaders need to reemphasize the timeline for implementation. Reforms require time for the mobilization of resources and for the acquisition of the technical skills necessary for improvement to occur.

When auditing your school or district, it is recommended that a leader consider the following informal approaches which allow for customization:

- School Systems "Cross Check": Identifies issues associated with alignment, attitude/atmosphere, accountability, and leadership (appendix A)

- Hierarchy of School/District Development: Assists in determining the current perception of staff regarding the school or district's improvement process (appendix A)
- QED Foundation: Involves an informal chart of transitional and transformational practices listed by category (chapter 6)
- Supplemental School and District Policy Review (appendix A)
- Curriculum Review: Examines the scope and quality of the curriculum, consistency, equity in the schools, program implementation, monitoring, and budget allocation[4]

The extent of the informal auditing process is highly individualized and contingent on the situational environment within a school or district. Revisions to informal instruments are possible without compromising the integrity of the audit. It should be further noted that there are formal audits that are commercially available, but adaptation is discouraged because it may impact its design integrity. Altering the instrument might affect its statistical model and inappropriately skew the results.

## STAGE 3: SCHOOL AND DISTRICT PLANNING

### System of Check and Balances

For effective planning and implementation to occur, a structure that incorporates a system of "checks and balances" is necessary to ensure functionality and effectiveness. School and district improvement teams are interconnected through the identification of priorities and the action plans that attempt to execute them. For example, if deemed a priority at the district level, the challenge of integrating equity should be present in both the district and school level plans. While the plans designed to effectuate the goal at the district level share the same common belief at the building level, there is latitude afforded in building a design that meets the uniqueness of each situation.

Effective goals are developed to address disconnections associated with the key foundational elements of instruction. Without having goals that include the elements of alignment, atmosphere, and accountability, the design will lack the substance required for successful and sustainable outcomes. It is therefore essential that each plan is reviewed and approved by the leadership at the district and building levels for inclusion of these elements.

Part of the review process should include scrutiny by instructional content supervisors. Since these individuals have "firsthand" knowledge of the curriculum design, these supervisors can provide quality input and suggestions for the plan. This review process involves members of the leadership team discussing the potential growth level for each building. The principal can seek adjustments based on situational data which is unique to the building.

This system of checks and balances builds internal integrity to goal development. It also enables a coalescing of support and resources. The potential "give and take" throughout the process builds a coalition that supports the action for implementation. Providing the superintendent with "veto power" over any aspect of the plan builds internal organizational accountability both vertically and horizontally.

## PLAN FOR REWARDS

Rewarding success and accommodating for potential failure is somewhat unusual for this process. Structuring an incentive program for meeting building goals is highly desirable. Much different from merit programs, the reward is shared by the building team for specific school improvement programs, which further empowers the staff in the process.

When goal setting requires "stretching" to reach achievement levels that are slightly beyond the grasp of a school, there is also a realization that all schools may not attain their targeted outcomes. Creating a safety net both financially and instructionally becomes important when schools are asked to take risks. This structure is basically a "fail safe" provision that allows a failing school to regroup and redirect efforts in the following year without devastating consequences. In the end, the program is designed to benefit all schools and all students.

## STAGE 4: ASSESSING PROGRESS

### Benchmarking Success

An improvement plan is only as good as the assessment process that is designed to review it. Continuous and periodic evaluation of the plan's effectiveness allows the school or district to adjust to unforeseen variables. Shifts resulting from legislative mandates or specific situational issues unique to a school or district are always a consideration.

If the plan is designed effectively, benchmarks permit for the periodic evaluation of progress. Like road markers, these indicators measure progress toward the target. They are the content-oriented indicators that connect the delivery of instruction to student proficiency.

If benchmarks are like distance markers, then the information gleaned from them is what drives the organization forward or requires it to "loop back" to reexamine specific content that was not quite understood. The more authentic the benchmark the more effective the remediation. This process eliminates the "lock step" lunge forward to the next unit. Gaps are minimized and no one is left behind when there are planned interventions to ensure mastery of content for all students.

The logical question is what happens to the students that understand the content? Are they not being penalized for their efforts? How will parents respond to reteaching and waiting for others to "catch up." And does remediation and regrouping stigmatize students?

For those students who are moving according to the designed pace of the curriculum, enrichment activities are designed that are commensurate with their ability. Creative building faculties regroup students temporarily until the reteaching is completed. They eventually rejoin the class to maintain its original heterogeneity.

While benchmarking and standardized testing have come under fire in recent years, creative solutions regarding student learning can balance meeting content substance and standards. This design recognizes the importance of providing each student with a proficient level of knowledge and skill. Proceeding without addressing a poorly delivered content unit or ignoring skill gaps will only exacerbate the performance issue in each school.

## PROFESSIONAL DEVELOPMENT

The assessment of progress may also highlight deficiencies with teaching practices and methodology. Not only does assessment chart a student's progress but it also provides data on how effectively the content is delivered. An improvement model that respects the professionalism of teachers and staff creates opportunities for continuous learning. These opportunities are highly individualized and designed to improve the "art of teaching."

Productive professional development involves a tiered system that respects various levels of teacher training. It is not punitive but rather supportive by accepting the reality that not every teacher requires the same level of professional development. With this design leaders view teacher development along a continuum of expertise.

Time in schools is a valued commodity. Competing factions are always attempting to carve out a slice of time for a new program or for a routine activity. By taking advantage of existing technology, access to training modules, speakers, and teaching methodology, learning can proceed anywhere or at any time of the day. It can keep the staff focused on its priority, quality instruction.

## REFLECTIVE QUESTIONS

- Identify an area of the school or district that thoroughly aligns with the organization's vision. Where is it disconnected?
- How has the leadership provided opportunities for inclusion in the improvement process?
- How has the school or district aligned equity into its academic plan?
- Do leadership goals reflect higher student achievement outcomes?
- Do evaluations reinforce the "status quo" or seek the implementation of transitional or transformational concepts?
- Is a system of "checks and balances" part of the improvement plan and approval process in your school or district? If so, explain.
- Have you considered a system of rewards for goal attainment? Why or why not?
- What type of audit would you recommend to "jump-start" the improvement process in your school or district? How would the school leadership gain support of the staff?
- How does your school or district ensure that all students acquire the knowledge and skills necessary to meet local or state standards?

## SUMMARY

- Organizational dynamics is a major factor in determining the outcome of any reform.
- "Synertegic" leadership understands how to build consensus within an organization.
- Leading an improvement initiative requires a thorough understanding of the teaching and learning process.
- Interrelated foundational elements drive the performance process forward toward improved student learning and achievement.
- Planning for increased performance involves a series of checks and balances that synergizes the leadership team to create a more targeted framework for improvement.
- A system of rewards accounts for both success and failure.
- Auditing focuses and delineates the action plans for improvement.
- Comprehensive auditing includes curriculum, practices, policy, communication leadership and aspirations.
- Progress is measured most accurately by school and district benchmarks that are authentic.
- Standards and substance matter.

## RECOMMENDATIONS

- Select an audit. See appendix B, "Leadership Training Module."
- Structure a framework for improvement.
- Develop a review and approval process.
- Create a system of rewards.
- Develop authentic benchmarks.
- Celebrate success.

## PROBLEM SOLVING

The school board of directors endorsed a philosophy that "good" was actually "good enough." The mayor of this small city scoffed at any additional investment in the schools by stating, "It was good enough for me, why shouldn't it be good enough for them?" Previously, this manufacturing city found itself inventing itself as a regional center for technology but the schools for the most part remained the same. The city also became a relocation center for refugees. The demographics of the school changed during the last 15 years. A walk through of the schools found buildings with "good bones" but overlooked routine maintenance caused several facility issues. Trash was often found stuck into the chain link fences on the property. The staff was dedicated and hardworking but seemed relegated to traditional instructional methodology. Everyone seemed overworked and tired. The superintendent retired. You have been selected for the job. Where do you begin and what are your long-range plans to move this district forward to meet the challenges of the 21st century? (Review chapters 1 through 7 to develop a plan.)

## NOTES

1. Malcolm Gladwell, *The Tipping Point: How Little Things Can Make a Big Difference* (New York: Little, Brown, 2000), 7.
2. Gladwell, *The Tipping Point*, 7.
3. Lisette Partelow and Sarah Shapiro, "Curriculum Reform in the Nation's Largest School Districts," *Center for American Progress*, August 28, 2018, https://americanprogress.org/issues/education-K-12-reports/2018/08/29/454704.
4. F. John Reh, "Pareto Principle or the 80/20 Rule," *Balance Careers*, October 23, 2019, https://www.thebalancecareers.com/pareto-s-principle-the-80-20-rule-2275148.

## Chapter 8

# Transformational Lessons

### CONSIDERATIONS

There are many factors to consider when a school or district determines the extent and depth of its improvement plan. In determining its framework or model, a school must recognize that such a decision is highly individualized and situationally based. Understanding and realistically assessing a school or district's current development along a continuum of improvement is crucial in this decision-making process.

The leap from a traditional learning process to a transformational platform is huge. Not every school or district is prepared or capable of making such a leap. It takes time, effort, and a consensus to do so. Depending on the depth of the identified learning deficiencies, a "synertegic" leader recognizes the importance of building the necessary groundwork before proceeding with such an ambitious agenda. Adept leaders know how to facilitate a gradual and continuous process toward the school or district's identified outcomes. Since internal conflict can disrupt even "the best of plans," leaders need to minimize the potential for it.

McREL International states that, "In continuous improvement systems, change occurs incrementally, as organizations learn from experience in testing and in refining strategies which produce better outcomes."[1] In schools and districts that are immersed in the process, "there is a cyclical approach to problem solving, allowing relevant actors to reflect on their work, identify problem areas, observe, evaluate and adapt interventions based on data collection."[2] Several popular improvement models that follow this process include:

- Plan, Do, Study, Act (PDSA)
- Sig Sigma (DMAIC)
- Results Oriented-Cycle of Inquiry (ROCI)
- Data Wise[3]

The continuous improvement model requires consideration of the following factors at the policy level:

- Fewer, specific, and measurable goals
- Flexibility
- Time
- Data use and capacity
- Evaluation
- Leadership
- Knowledge sharing
- Capacity building
- Stakeholder investment

The Oregon Department of Education focuses on improving outcomes through the following process:

- Determining what is working and what needs to change
- Establishing a process to engage stakeholders to reflect change
- Leveraging effective practices to implement a plan
- Using data to monitor and make timely adjustments to the improved outcomes[4]

Research for Better Teaching stresses the "importance of sustainable achievement, professional development, monitoring, and high-leverage intervention."[5] By focusing on the "whole student" through "identified priorities such as teaching and learning, family, community partnerships, school culture, and operational effectiveness,"[6] Hartford Public Schools generated its goals to increase ESL proficiency and decrease absenteeism.

The Council of Chief School Officers, through its identification process for schools in need of "comprehensive or targeted support, examines data points that illustrate academic deficiencies in Title I schools."[7] Graduation rates and prolonged years of underperformance are the criteria for identification, along with disciplinary rates for suspension and chronic absenteeism.

While the model for each school or district varies, the challenge of determining exactly what to improve is even more important. Identifying the wrong learning priority will scuttle any plan to improve. A poorly designed assessment measure, whether selected through a lack of expertise or randomness, when combined with succumbing to misguided agendas, will continue the "status quo" of poor performance well into the future.

Catherine Matthews of Everett Public Schools indicated that success or failure of a plan is about "wanting information that is actionable and helps us solve the right problem. Gathering data that aligns with the district's strategic plan to produce students with grit, a growth mind-set, a sense of belonging and social awareness involves asking the right questions."[8] Finding effective interventions are a result of a well thought out process. Aligning the building action plans to the district's strategic goal is critical as Everett attempts to reach higher outcomes.

When assessing for improvement, all the processes, practices, and structures are comparatively analyzed in relation to well-defined performance criteria that will identify disconnections that lead to systemic underachievement. Without connecting the identified deficiencies to systemic disconnections associated with the organizational elements of alignment, atmosphere/attitude (culture), accountability, and adept leadership, most plans for increased performance will fail to reach the targeted outcomes.[9] Linking these elements to the identified priorities increases coherence, consistency, and performance outcomes.

## CASE STUDIES

Several case studies are provided to illustrate how differently schools and districts approach the process of improvement. Some districts conduct a systemic analysis while others isolate a deficiency and incorporate remediation into the fabric of the school or district. Each framework has strengths, but each should be critiqued in the context of its focus and the plan's potential impact on student achievement.

## CASE STUDY #1

Queen Anne's County Public School System in Maryland used the Middle States Commission on Elementary and Secondary Schools' "Excellence by Design" (2010)[10] as its framework for improvement. A System Planning Team identified priorities through a self-reflection process by asking the following questions:

- What are the gaps between what we say in our Profile of Graduates regarding what we want our graduates to know, be able to do with what they know, and/or what student qualities and performance we want them to demonstrate?
- Which of the gaps constitute the highest priorities for narrowing if we are to move closer over the next seven years to achieving our mission?
- Are there areas of our system's capacity that must be improved in order to improve our students' performance to the levels we desire and expect?

The district aligned its objectives with the targeted results to mirror the anticipated growth in achievement during the next seven years. The goals were also aligned with the district's mission. The development of the district's "Blueprint for Excellence" was partially to comply with the state's requirement to develop a strategic plan for growth and improvement. In doing so, the framework for this plan included goals, processes, and supports for "all students." The conceptual plan included the following:

- A clear and shared focus
- High standards and expectations
- Effective leadership
- Collaboration and communication
- Alignment with state standards
- Monitoring of teaching and learning
- Focused professional development
- Supportive learning environment
- Family and community involvement

In executing this plan, district strategies included but were not limited to the following:

- Implementing curriculum, instruction, and assessments that aligned with state standards
- Engaging teacher teams in technology-supported, data-driven decision-making within the collaborative school cultures
- Embedding high-quality, focused professional development.
- Seeking a high level of stakeholder involvement.

Student performance content area goals focused on the following areas:

- Fine and practical arts
- Diversity within its gifted and talented population
- Proficiency at all levels involving math, reading, world languages, science, social studies, world of work
- Increasing diversity among its staff
- Technology for administrative and parent communication
- Reduction of disciplinary incidents
- Improvement of community outreach

A major component of the plan involved improving teacher and principal effectiveness, teacher induction/mentoring, and the equitable distribution of effective staff. The final component of the plan involved "turning around" the lowest achieving schools.

## CASE STUDY #2

The Oakland Unified School District (California) approached the issue of transformation differently. After experiencing initiatives associated with "No Child Left Behind" and "Race to the Top," the school district decided to implement a social emotional learning (SEL) program as the means to improve academic success. The district's vision was not limited to stand-alone curricula kits, but rather to link the initiative to all aspects of the district. The process began with a small number of district office personnel. The group included those in key leadership positions, some academics, and a few principals. The team met for a month to discuss and intentionally practice SEL competencies.

Since the school district recognized that the SEL initiative was essentially a top-down mandate, they chose to focus on educating every adult about SEL and to involve them in the rollout. They also understood that it would take time to implement SEL practices into daily practices. For integration to occur, the adults needed to go through their own learning processes.

Stage 1 of the district's implementation process included the following:

- Identifying needs: In a district with high levels of crime, violence, and poverty, the students encountered tremendous social and emotional barriers at school.
- Making a long-term commitment: A five-year plan was created.
- Starting with the adults: They started by educating every adult and then involving them in the rollout.
- Including everyone: The school district involved the unions and struggled for a cross-cultural perspective.

According to the design team, the most challenging aspect of the plan involved building diverse representation and content. As a result of this cultural lens, content included race, class, gender identity, discrimination, age, and language. By focusing on these issues, trust was created. Marginalized voices now realized that they had something to offer to the process.

Stage 2 of the process included the following:

- Weaving SEL into the culture and curricula: The district integrated the vision at every level, making it part of the implementation of the Common Core.

- Keeping the eye on the prize: Teacher-leaders met quarterly to discuss and practice SEL integration and share what they learned with their staff at their school sites.
- Creating infrastructure: The district provided professional development, adopted new curriculum materials, and developed an alternative measurement system.

The SEL group of teacher-leaders met quarterly to discuss, practice, and understand the integration of SEL into the fabric of the school and district.

## CASE STUDY #3

In 2001, a suburban school district in southeastern Pennsylvania was underperforming. Despite significant resources and an enviable per pupil expenditure, student achievement never met the expectations of the community. For years, the school's board of directors sought solutions to the issue and even embraced a merit pay plan for teachers. The school board embraced a merit pay plan that was developed through a grant from the Pennsylvania Department of Education, in conjunction with the University of Pennsylvania. In determining the "value-added" contribution to yearly learning, researchers developed a formula with 26 factors that identified a teacher's value-added. In the end there was little agreement among stakeholders regarding the accuracy of the growth factor attributed to each teacher. The stakeholders agreed that the merit pay plan generated an atmosphere of contentiousness between the teachers and the school board.

With contract negotiations stalled concerning the merit pay plan, both sides agreed to a plan that focused on increasing student achievement by systemically improving the district's instruction. With salary and personnel issues decided, the union leadership met with the superintendent to develop a framework to improve student performance. The framework, "Reaching Above and Beyond," included the development of district goals, building goals, district and building improvement teams, a review and approval process, and a reward program, as well as a Master Teacher Program. The plan became a negotiated part of the contract that remains in force today.

Unique to the plan is a system of checks and balances modeled after those in the U.S. Constitution, designed to check the power of each branch of government. Plans were developed at various organizational levels and were subject to checks or review by principals, curriculum staff members, and the central office. The superintendent had veto power over decisions at any level but judiciously reserved the use of that authority.

Aside from having goals developed by those on the "front lines" in conjunction with those at the district level, the plan created a high level of participation by all staff members. Principals and school improvement teams negotiated rates of projected student growth with the central office based on situational factors in their buildings. Every aspect of the plan "fit like a glove."

The plan recognized the interdependence of learning upon many factors. The plan also was cognizant of connecting the key elements of instruction for cohesion, consistency, and maximum outcomes. "All students" and "all subgroups" were considered essential in maximizing potential.

By 2010, the school district had been recognized for its ongoing achievement and systemic improvement. While the name of the plan may have changed, the principles of the plan remain intact.

## CASE STUDY #4

From their inception, charter schools were designed as schools of choice. As of 2018–2019, there were approximately 7,486 charter schools in the United States.[11] They are more autonomous because there is greater flexibility in areas of operation and management than those requirements mandated in traditional public schools. The design also provides them with the opportunity for greater experimentation. Key principles of charter schools generally involve the following:

- Maintain good management and consistent stable leadership focusing on student achievement, cost efficiency, and fiscal accountability
- Emphasize academic rather than nonacademic goals, plus high expectations for students and staff
- Implement rigorous standards-based curricula
- Use a longer school day and year
- Hire smart teachers based on top academic records and/or subject related experience, not simple possession of a regular teaching credential
- Create grade-level teams of teachers to analyze data, plan for interventions, and design instruction
- Test students often and use results as diagnostic tools to spot student weaknesses
- Prevent grade inflation by comparing grades with test scores
- Use teacher methods that are empirically proven to improve student performance
- Ensure classroom accountability through frequent classroom visits by the principal

- Promote high-quality teaching through rigorous evaluations with tough consequences for poor performance
- Expect students to behave in a manner conducive to learning
- Implement innovative school schedules/student groupings[12]

Charters were created to transform the educational landscape. Action-learning research and experimentation were encouraged from their inception and incorporated into their design.

Mastery Charter Schools (PA) is an institution that focuses on underperforming schools and regions with the intent of "turning around" the quality of the education program in those areas. Currently, the Mastery Charter serves more than 14,000 students in 24 Philadelphia schools. Many of those students meet the definition of economically disadvantaged.

Mastery Charter–Thomas Campus is a high-performing college preparatory "turnaround school" serving 710 students in grades 7 through 12. The graduating class was approximately 110. The school's composition includes 70 percent economically disadvantaged, 21 percent special education, and 11 percent English language learners (ELL). The school provides an array of honors and advanced placement courses, along with a variety of clubs and activities. The school followed the Mastery Charter instructional plan and goals as follows:

- Prepare students to pursue their dreams: Provide a program rich in critical thinking and a rigorous curriculum delivered by passionate teachers
- Provide a strong academic design: Offer engaging and participatory instruction that is also relation driven
- Prepare students for success after graduation: Expand curriculum offerings and provide dual enrollment classes that result in an associate degree
- Provide family and community engagement: Consider families as partners in the teaching and learning process[13]

According to the school's 2019–2020 college profile, students were admitted to more than 200 colleges and institutions of higher learning.

## CASE STUDY #5

The Atlanta School District (Georgia) took a unique approach to school improvement. While the implemented plan (2002–2003) is older, it is relevant because it focused on the role of the central office in improving performance. Reorganization of the central office is often structural and related to the district's organizational chart. What makes this reorganization unusual is that it focuses on the actual work of the district office.

According to the superintendent, the central office reflected the disarray that existed in the organization. The central office was totally removed from immediate contact with schools and not necessarily focused on the kinds of work practices that promised to improve teaching and learning, particularly in Atlanta's mostly African American and low-income neighborhoods. In conjunction with the Wallace Foundation, the district improvement plan focused on the following overall goals:

- Connecting directly the work at the central office to teaching and learning
- Engaging the entire central office in reform
- Remaking work practices and their relationships with schools to support teaching and learning[14]

To further these goals, instructional dimensions of the central office transformation were identified. These dimensions focused on learning partnerships with principals to deepen a school's instructional practice. By providing principals with direct instructional support, principals would have the resources and skill to build internal capacity. Rather than contracting with external groups for support, assistance is delivered directly by central office administrators. Specific central office leaders were designated as instructional support directors (ISD) who focused 100 percent of their time on improving the principal's instructional practice.

Professional development was provided to the ISDs to assist them with instructional methodology, group engagement techniques, modeling, and coaching. A case management approach was applied to the ISD's assignment. Each ISD became an expert on the specific needs, strengths, goals, and character for each school assigned to them. They became responsible for delivering services and solving problems for each school on their case load.

For central office leaders who want to engage in central office transformation, it was recommended that the work begin by executing the following steps:

- Develop a theory of action for how the central office practice will contribute to improving teaching and learning, and plan to revise this theory as the work unfolds
- Invest substantially in people to lead the work throughout the central office, especially at the interface between the central office and the schools

- Engage key stakeholders, political supporters, and potential funders in understanding that central office transformation is important and requires sustained commitment[15]

The Wallace Foundation, which replicated this approach in three large urban school districts, indicated that it demonstrates the value of using the central office in building internal capacity. Some consideration was previously given to outsourcing many of the functions performed at the central office. This approach has illustrated the "untapped potential" that exists internally in a school district.

## CASE STUDY #6

A school district in Texas consisting of approximately 53,000 students in 67 schools serves an economically challenged Hispanic population that includes significant percentages of free and reduced lunch, limited English proficiency, and special education students. It routinely struggled in meeting state mandates.

Self-described as working in "silos," teachers were handed the keys to their classrooms and left to work largely in isolation. School teams worked together on community-building events but rarely met to discuss student achievement. They appeared to lack a focus on collaboration and shared goals.

The first step in its improvement process involved building collaboration. The improvement framework focused on building Professional Learning Communities (PLC). Being a large district, the initiative took time to develop and implement. Building a common language was essential in creating the PLCs. Slowly the focus shifted from getting through the curriculum to discussing what students needed to be successful. The district also targeted the following areas for improvement in the next five years:

- Providing a rigorous and meaningful curriculum by creating integrated learning experiences to meet individual student needs ensuring students are future ready
- Promoting college, career, and military preparation and readiness using systems and structures
- Recruiting and retaining highly qualified staff
- Using a culturally responsive approach for stakeholder engagement
- Establishing safe schools with social and emotional programming
- Promoting an exemplary learning environment through established and innovative practices[16]

In year one of the program, the district demonstrated significant increases in emergent literacy skills and mathematics proficiency.

## REFLECTIVE QUESTION

- Which case studies provided immediate improvement, sustained improvement, systemic reform, and transformational change?

## SUMMARY

The six case studies provided in this chapter illustrate the highly individualized nature of school transformation. It is not "one size fits all." Rather, it is based on situational factors in each school or district. These case studies should not be viewed as exemplars for success, but instead as examples of how each district struggled to find a solution to its achievement issue. Each study has merit, as well as inherent weaknesses. The challenge lies in the identification of disconnections and obstacles that, when effectively remediated, will make a significant difference in student performance.

Some of the case studies highlight implementing or integrating a program or concept into the fabric of a school or district. While embedding the program into the organization's framework for improvement is highly desirable, this singular action will not guarantee that student achievement will improve. Successful plans recognize the interconnection of achievement factors and the development of goals/action plans in a cohesive and effective manner.

The efficacy of a plan to transform a school or district is related to connecting the key organizational elements to instructional actions that create the desired change and are sustainable over time. "Synertegic" leaders recognize the complexity of learning and they also understand what is needed to improve it. Stand-alone solutions that operate independently do not have the instructional tentacles necessary to improve overall achievement.

Successful systemic improvement always involves the key organizational components of alignment, creating a productive and resilient atmosphere, accountability, and adept leadership. Integration of an idea or plan is a good step, but creating interconnections between the district's vision, instructional initiatives, actions, and policy generates internal capacity, cohesiveness, and consistency.

## RECOMMENDATIONS

- Identify situational factors in your school or district that require consideration in transforming instruction and learning in your district.
- Prioritize instructional factors that are key to teaching and learning.
- Identify obstacles to the learning process that, if eliminated, will immediately "pave the way" to higher achievement. (Identify the factors in a student's life that a school or district can control.)
- Select design components that are necessary for inclusion in an improvement plan to transform achievement.
- Outline a framework to improve school or district student performance.

## PROBLEM SOLVING

Read the conclusion and determine the status of your school or district in terms of student achievement. Determine how you as a school leader will position your school or district to meet the challenges on the horizon.

## NOTES

1. Jane Best and Allison Dunlap, "Continuous Improvement in Schools and Districts: Policy Considerations," *McRel International*, October 2020, p. 1, https://files.eric.ed.gov/fulltext/ED557599.pdf.

2. Best and Dunlap, "Continuous Improvement in Schools and Districts," p. 2.

3. S. Park, S. Hironaka, P. Carver, and L. Nordstrum, "Continuous Improvement in Education," *Carnegie Foundation for the Advancement of Teaching*, 2013, https://carnegiefoundation.org/sites/default/files/carnegie-foundation_continuous-improvement-2013.05.pdf.

4. "Continuous Improvement Process and Planning," *Oregon Department of Education*, modified March 25, 2021, https://www.oregon.gov/ode/schools-and-districts.

5. "Empowering Sustainable School Improvement—Our Approach," *Research for Better Teaching*, 2016, https://www.rbteach.com/why-rbt/ourapproach.

6. "District Model for Excellence—Strategic Plan 2018–2022," *Hartford Public Schools*, https://www.hartfordschools.org/districtmodel/

7. Tony Evers and Chris Minnich, "School and District FAQs, Topic 1: Identification of Schools," *Council of Chief State Officers*, 2016, p. 1, https://www.ccsso.org/sites/default/files/2017-12/SDI_FAQ_Topic_1-_Identification_of_Schools_09062016.pdf.

8. "Success Stories Everett," *Second Step*, 2017, https://www.secondstep.org/success-stories/everett.

9. Vincent F. Cotter and Robert Hassler, *Performance Is Key: Connecting the Links to Leadership and Excellence* (Lanham, MD: Rowman & Littlefield, 2018).

10. Middle States Commissions on Elementary and Secondary Schools, "Excellence by Design—Queen Anne's County Public Schools Self Study Report: The Plan for Growth and Improvement," February 10, 2010.

11. "What Is a Charter School?" *National Charter School Resource Center*, September 13, 2018, https://charterschoolcenter.ed.gov/what-charter-school.

12. Lance T. Izumi, "What Works: Inside Model Charter Schools," *Center on Innovation and Improvement-Academic Development Institute*, 2008, http://www.centerii.org/search/resources/whatworksmodelcharter.pdf.

13. "Welcome to Mastery Schools," *Master Schools*, https://masterycharter.org

14. Meredith I. Honig, Michael A. Copland, Lydia Rainey, and Morena Newton, "Central Office Transformation for District-Wide Teaching and Learning Improvement," commissioned by the Wallace Foundation: Center for the Study of Teaching and Policy (Seattle: University of Washington, April 2010).

15. Honig, Copland, Rainey, and Newton, "Central Office Transformation for District-Wide Teaching and Learning Improvement."

16. "Strategic Plan 2020–2025," *Pasadena Independent School District*, https://pasadenaisd.org.

*Chapter 9*

# Getting "It" Right

There are "lines in the sand" that cannot be crossed or abandoned when committing to school reform. Doing so substantively reduces the quality of the initiative. Violating them erodes one's ability to lead by compromising the validity of the reform.

## ELIMINATING THE "THEATER OF REFORM"

Change, reform, and certainly transformation require courage and skill. Getting "it" right the first time can often chart a school's trajectory for years. Getting "it" wrong could threaten its very existence. Substantive change is rarely initiated at the "grassroots" level. Institutions have an internal organizational virus that fights to maintain the "status quo." Directives that seek to change the "status quo" usually emanate from external sources or when an internal leader has been directed to do so.

Only through collaborative deliberation, due diligence, and consensus building will an initiative for reform have a chance of survival. The rate of survival is determined by the facilitative and "synertegic" skills of the organization's leader. Leaders who lack the ability, knowledge, or facilitative skill opt for the "theater of reform" rather than substantive change. These leaders are the pretenders of reform. They are the well-intentioned "snake oil" barkers of the midway that make a lot of noise but produce little. They suggest "packaged" programs as solutions and offer excuses for poor performance but always seek more funding to accomplish the reform. They are the schmoozers who slap the backs of stakeholders but offer little in return. They are generally liked because they do not "rock the boat" even when students are not prepared for the future.

Too often these leaders create an improvement process that is couched in slogans, rallies, brochures, and nomenclature designed to motivate, inflate egos, or showcase peripheral talent. While it may build a "feel-good" atmosphere, substantive growth in achievement rarely occurs unless it is tied to a program of rigor, expectations, and standards. Changes in terminology, gimmicks, or administrative pontification do not produce results. Focus, hard work, commitment, and skilled leadership do.

## KNOWLEDGE

The pursuit of knowledge has long been regarded as one of learning's highest principles. Possessing content knowledge, internally understanding it, and externally demonstrating it are considered the keys to universal learning. Any attempts to erode a factual body of knowledge or degrade its content are foolish, at best. Leaders are sometimes pressured to "lower the bar" so that more students can experience success. Succumbing to this pressure results in false gratification that is short-lived in a global society.

Rather than lower expectations and drive instruction to the middle, "raising" everyone to meet higher expectations through engaging methodologies appears preferable because it will produce higher outcomes for more students. By creating an age-appropriate climate reflective of knowledge acquisition based on standards and verified through norm-based testing, comparative growth can be measured. Substantive learning takes place when there is rigor, high expectations, and verification of learning. Ignoring these ingredients reverts the reform effort back to the theater of "smoke and mirrors." Creating an illusion of achievement that is not norm referenced in a world that values knowledge, skill, and talent is simply fraudulent.

## FACT AND TRUTH

The quality of any reform is based on the decisions a leader makes. Basing decisions on fact and research squashes the potential of opinionated narratives. Efforts to change the "status quo" are prone to manipulation by those with agendas related to power and control, skewed philosophies that benefit "the few," or ideological narratives that exclude proven practices and curriculum materials that generate intellectual curiosity and thinking.

Leaders require the fortitude to connect validated research and practice in a manner that guides the decision-making process toward higher level outcomes for all children. Respecting diverse opinion is part of the process but allowing unsubstantiated opinion undue influence on the change process is tantamount to educational pollution. Without clarity of purpose the reform descends into a cloud of mediocrity. The inconvenient truths behind knowledge, learning, and practice should prevail in an atmosphere that is transparent and upholds a mantra that children come first.

## BALANCE

A pendulum swings both to the right and the left. It seldom stops in the middle unless it loses momentum or its kinetic energy. It is a function of space, time, and such forces as gravity. Educational reform is similar in that it is also subject to the forces of time and power.

The swings in the reform movement move along a continuum that is impacted by politics, economics, legislation, ideology, and the media. Often, the loudest voices are heard. At its worst, reformers seek to purge existing knowledge, learning and practice from the lexicon of good practice. In its haste to change the "status quo," research-based pedagogy and methodology are removed to make way for the unproven new and different.

The challenge of "finding a balance" of "what works" measured against the potential of the unknown is formidable. Having the knowledge to determine the difference between successful proven practice and the proposed hyperbole for change helps to eliminate any narrative that may define the reform as superficial or uninformed. Yielding to undocumented and unproven solutions will leave the passengers on this journey stranded and confused when they are eventually confronted with the reality of real knowledge, skill, and competition.

An inclusionary, customized, and balanced approach to reform understands the situational nature of reform and the nuance required to accomplish it. A "scorched earth" process rarely works. Finesse, focus, and balance are vital, but it is the voice of "synertegic" leadership that "eliminates the theater" and delivers substantive change.

## RESPONSIBILITY

Bill Parcels, former professional football coach, stated, "You are what your record says you are."[1] Yes, the buck does stop with you! You can make all the excuses for failure you want, but, ultimately, if you do not improve student achievement, it is your responsibility to "own it." It becomes your legacy. As a leader, you must assume responsibility for permitting internal systems and known obstacles to achievement to remain in place. Your role is not to blame others, but to lead them to make changes that positively impact the lives of students who have been entrusted to them.

## REFLECTIVE QUESTIONS

- What is the source of any internal turmoil in your school or district? What can you do improve it?
- Does the leadership "cave" to unfounded internal or external pressure?
- Do you own the existing school or district's achievement level? If not, who does?

## RECOMMENDATIONS

- Eliminate the "theater of reform" by adopting a substantive improvement plan.
- Establish a process for the addition or removal of curriculum materials.
- Understand the research and methods that attempt to improve the performance for all students.
- Identify the proven practices that work. Eliminate those that do not.

## PROBLEM SOLVING

A parent group wants to remove a renowned literary classic from the school district's curriculum. A much larger group opposes its removal. As the leader of the district, how do you navigate this issue?

## NOTE

1. Ben Hunt, "You Are What Your Record Says You Are," *Epsilon Theory*, November 3, 2018, https://www.epsilontheory.com/you-are-what-your-record-says-you-are/.

# Conclusion

Based on the extent of the issues confronting U.S. public-school systems, there are those among us that believe that the "sun is setting" on the viability of a public education. The dark shadow of lagging student achievement has dogged the imagination of public schools for more than a decade. Most recently, the image has been tarnished by school closures and the subsequent loss of learning during the pandemic.

Despite the valiant efforts of school personnel to provide a semblance of normality during the pandemic, the learning loss appeared to impact the psyche of the country. Not only were students falling behind academically, but also systemic issues that existed for years were amplified. Recovery from the pandemic and our ability to rectify long-standing obstacles in the instructional process will determine whether the "sun is truly setting" or "rising" over our cherished educational process.

Throughout our country's history, we have confronted crisis and uncertainty with resilience, vigor, and with an openness to reinvention. Our national optimism gives us the opportunity to solve complex problems. It drives sustainable solutions to our current academic deficiencies. Public schools have accomplished so much during our history. The "masses" were efficiently educated in institutions that met the demands of an era. A new era has arrived so *now* is the time to restructure for success.

For the "sun to shine" on public education, we must move beyond our current "status quo" approach to learning and restructure the delivery of instruction to confront inequality, deficiencies in technological infrastructure, civic involvement, and the social-emotional well-being of "All" students. While these challenges appear daunting, we have the collective talent in our schools to restructure and build a better future for "All" students. We simply need the "will" to get it done.

Inherent in meeting these challenges in this post–COVID-19 era is having unrelenting leadership that "Leans into the Future." Forward leaning leadership does not shy away from challenges. Rather, it learns from the past and designs for the future. It strategizes, synergizes, and finds a path to success. It values knowledge, research, skills, and fact.

In transforming schools and school districts, the leadership team must possess the skills to facilitate change in a complex organization. Minimizing internal conflict through stakeholder inclusion is critical. For leaders, having a deep understanding of the teaching and learning process is essential in identifying priorities that will transform the instructional culture.

It should be remembered that transformation is complex and evolutionary. It is a systemic process which involves incremental change. Genuine growth transpires when data identifies the internal disconnections that are the real obstacles to achievement. Authentic data that is actionable focuses the organization on what and how to improve. Connecting the data, goals, and action plans to the overarching organizational elements (alignment, atmosphere, accountability, and adept leadership) results in a plan with higher efficacy. Consistency in the execution of a plan generates cross district, and cross grade level outcomes.

Transformational reform touches every component of a school or district. Singular action to correct a problem is simply insufficient when seeking solutions to such complex issues as underperformance or consistent school failure. Systemic disconnections are frequently interrelated and impact learning outcomes. Too frequently they are deeply embedded in an organization's traditions.

Changing an organization that is entrenched in ineffective traditional practices is a bold path for educators to take. Minimally, it will commit a school or district to self-reflection. The ability to objectively critique all aspects of an educational program might remove its façade of excellence. Taking the next step to a transitional plan opens the door to genuine improvement. Transformational change will only occur when we recognize that student learning is paramount.

Recouping COVID-19 learning loss is possible with proven strategies, interventions, and "out of the box" thinking. Returning to "normalcy" or a "new normal" ignores rectifying the systemic issues that have hampered student achievement for far too long. Changing long-standing issues, often complicated by politics, economics, and other institutional issues, requires a moral imperative that recognizes that if the performance of "all" children rises, so will the future of our country.

# Appendix A
## *Performance Assessment Instruments*

This section features four instruments. They are as follows:

1. The *School Systems "Cross Check"* is used to determine the status of a school or district's level of performance in accordance with organizational elements and the extent of adherence to them. Additional analysis is provided regarding existing documents and policies. This instrument yields information regarding overall organizational cohesion. The instrument provides a level of effectiveness.
2. An *Abbreviated "Cross Check" Instrument* provides a "quick" survey of areas that are systemically important.
3. A *Document Review and Analysis* examines departmental and operational practices which informally correlate to higher outcomes and quality.
4. A *Hierarchy of School Development* provides stakeholders with the opportunity to self-assess developmental levels of performance. This informal assessment provides a baseline for growth along with providing performance categories.

### A-1: SCHOOL SYSTEMS "CROSS CHECK": EVALUATION INSTRUMENT (REVISED EDITION 2021)

### Background

The School Systems "Cross Check" examines the interconnection of school and district processes and programs by "cross checking" embedded performance threads in key organizational areas. The key elements and organizational threads examined in the "Cross Check" instrument include the following:

- Alignment
- Atmosphere/attitude or culture
- Accountability
- Adept leadership

The School Systems "Cross Check" attempts to research an organization for the existence of key elemental threads by identifying tangible, concrete demonstrations of those threads and providing a framework to make recommendations that will result in a more effective organization.

## Directions

Rank responses to the questions of each of the four areas (alignment, atmosphere/attitude, accountability, and adept leadership) as high (3), moderate (2), or low (1). For example:

- A high ranking (3) indicates a high prevalence, presence, or existence of a *characteristic or term* identified in the question.
- A moderate ranking (2) indicates a moderate prevalence, presence, or existence of a *characteristic or term* identified in the question.
- A low ranking (1) indicates little existence or presence of the identified *characteristic or term* in the question.

## Definitions

*Student Achievement* ("SA") refers to student performance in academic and instructional areas.

*Leadership* involves the superintendent, principal, assistant principal, supervisor, and others identified as school administrators or part of configured leadership teams.

*School, School District, District* are organizational educational units.

## Alignment

Focus: All practices, processes, and goals are aligned from the "boardroom" to the classroom.

1. The district uses a *comprehensive instructional plan* as a framework in the development of the organization's goals. 1–2–3

2. The district conducts an *annual review* of existing programs for effectiveness. 1–2–3
3. The district developed *measurable goals* with timelines for completion. 1–2–3
4. Annual *district goals are aligned* with building goals. 1–2–3
5. The district's *values, mission, and vision* match behaviors exhibited by its members. 1–2–3
6. The district is committed to *continuous improvement*. 1–2–3
7. The district assesses its *strengths and weaknesses* annually. 1–2–3
8. The district created *informal classroom assessments* aligned to its instructional goals. 1–2–3
9. The district is *focused* on improving identified instructional issues. 1–2–3
10. The *noninstructional components* of the district support student achievement. 1–2–3
11. The district plans include a *multi-year plan* for improvement. 1–2–3
12. The district *reviews procedures and processes* that impact student achievement. 1–2–3
13. The *"day-to-day" work* of the district addresses student achievement. 1–2–3
14. The district *approved instructional programs* are improving student achievement. 1–2–3
15. Leaders make the improvement of *student achievement a priority*. 1–2–3
16. Teaching reflects *District and School Action Plans* to improve student achievement. 1–2–3
17. *District and School Action Plans* are effective in improving student achievement. 1–2–3
18. Members of the district appear to *understand district targets and outcomes*. 1–2–3
19. There is a belief that the district has the *internal capacity* to improve. 1–2–3
20. There is an *expectation* that the district can overcome its student achievement issues. 1–2–3
21. The district utilizes *instructional benchmarks* to access its progress. 1–2–3
22. The improvement process is *inclusive and collaborative*. 1–2–3
23. The staff is *empowered* to create and implement solutions to problems. 1–2–3
24. Staff members have an avenue to *participate* in instructional decisions. 1–2–3

25. Staff members *understand* the parts of *the plan* that impact them directly. 1–2–3

**Attitude/Atmosphere/Culture**

Focus: To build a culture of teamwork, collaboration, and positive attitude that maximizes the talents of employees in creating a high performing organization.

1. Staff members demonstrate the *values* of the organization. 1–2–3
2. The district encourages *professional development*. 1–2–3
3. *Adequate time* has been provided for *collaboration*. 1–2–3
4. A *problem-solving framework* is utilized. 1–2–3
5. District *practices empower* staff. 1–2–3
6. New staff exhibit the *desired attitude, personality, and aptitude*. 1–2–3
7. New staff possess skills that *align with the district's challenges and goals*. 1–2–3
8. The *placement of staff* is based on skills and strengths. 1–2–3
9. The district has the *"right people on the bus."* 1–2–3
10. Staff members work *collaboratively* to meet district and building goals. 1–2–3
11. The district is a *team working* toward a common goal. 1–2–3
12. There is a strong sense of *"buy-in"* in meeting goals. 1–2–3
13. The district fosters a *mentoring and coaching model* for staff. 1–2–3
14. The district supports a *differentiated model* of professional development. 1–2–3
15. The district supports a *"teacher leader" instructional model* for program. 1–2–3
16. A *career ladder* is provided for those teachers interested in learning opportunities. 1–2–3
17. Members of the organization are *recognized for performance* in the classroom. 1–2–3
18. Staff members collaborate to improve *instructional practice*. 1–2–3
19. *Professional Development* is aligned with district goals and practices. 1–2–3
20. The district provides *adequate resources* to improve achievement. 1–2–3
21. A *"child-first"* mantra is pervasive. 1–2–3
22. The organization views *instruction as a priority*. 1–2–3
23. The staff *defers individual accolades to one of group recognition*. 1–2–3
24. Leaders instill *confidence that success is possible*. 1–2–3

25. There is a climate of *"shared responsibility."* 1–2–3

## Accountability

Focus: To design a systemic, customized, continuous improvement model with measurable benchmark indicators and processes that monitor and adjust effectiveness.

1. The district consistently meets its *targeted outcomes.* 1–2–3
2. The district has a *system of accountability.* 1–2–3
3. The district holds *individuals accountable* for achievement results. 1–2–3
4. The district has a *group system of accountability* (i.e., building, department, etc.). 1–2–3
5. The district's system of *accountability motivates me* to improve student achievement. 1–2–3
6. *Data gathering is focused* on student performance. 1–2–3
7. The district has a *design* that includes achievement focused goals. 1–2–3
8. Goals and Expectations are *communicated.* 1–2–3
9. Building Goals are *derived* from District Goals. 1–2–3
10. All goals are measured with *specific criteria.* 1–2–3
11. Action Plans *assign responsibility* for measurement and completion. 1–2–3
12. *Multiple sources of data* (i.e., standardized tests, benchmarks, etc.) assess progress. 1–2–3
13. Data is *reviewed quarterly and/or annually.* 1–2–3
14. Data reports and summaries are *provided to the staff and community.* 1–2–3
15. Data is utilized to *adjust, and make corrections* as needed. 1–2–3
16. Accountability includes *what* is taught, *how* it is taught, and student *results.* 1–2–3
17. Accountability includes *teacher goals*, which involves student progress. 1–2–3
18. Classroom *Experimentation* and *Action Research* are encouraged. 1–2–3
19. The system of accountability includes *interventions* for struggling teachers. 1–2–3
20. The evaluation process *encourages professional growth.* 1–2–3
21. The staff is *proficient in measuring* student achievement. 1–2–3
22. The staff is *proficient in the analysis* of data and utilizes it to improve achievement. 1–2–3

23. A data system links student reports and data in planning for *resource allocation*. 1–2–3
24. Classroom *observations* are helpful in *improving performance*. 1–2–3
25. *Evaluations* provide feedback that *improves teaching and learning*. 1–2–3

## Adept Leadership

Focus: To develop a collaborative model that assists in aligning every aspect of the organization to achieve higher performance and excellence.

1. The leadership team *facilitated the goal development* process. 1–2–3
2. The leadership *reviewed long and short-term action plans*. 1–2–3
3. The leadership team *reinforces the values and beliefs* of the district. 1–2–3
4. The leadership team, as part of the review process, *eliminated ineffective programs*. 1–2–3
5. The leadership team *eliminated non-instructional distractions*. 1–2–3
6. The leadership is *"laser-focused" on achievement* and improvement. 1–2–3
7. The leadership team *inspires the district's personnel* to improve. 1–2–3
8. *Flexibility* is exhibited in implementing goals and action plans. 1–2–3
9. Leaders are *inclusive* in the *decision-making process*. 1–2–3
10. Leaders *encourage "risk taking"* or "out-of-the box" thinking. 1–2–3
11. Leaders *engage all stakeholders* (i.e., teachers, parents, students, etc.). 1–2–3
12. Leaders *seek additional resources* to assist in the improvement process. 1–2–3
13. Leaders *reinforce teamwork*. 1–2–3
14. The leaders of the organization *value the people within it*. 1–2–3
15. Leaders *encourage staff members* to grow professionally. 1–2–3
16. The leadership team is *inclusive in its problem-solving process*. 1–2–3
17. The leadership *communicates effectively* with all staff members. 1–2–3
18. Leaders *model the values, beliefs, and mission* of the district. 1–2–3
19. The leadership *organized frameworks*, structures, or processes to ensure success. 1–2–3
20. Leaders assume *responsibility for the success* or shortcomings of the district. 1–2–3
21. Leaders demonstrated *expertise in the execution* of district or school goals. 1–2–3
22. Leaders have developed a well-articulated *parent engagement program*. 1–2–3

23. The leadership created an *environment for students and staff to succeed.* 1–2–3
24. The leadership team operates in a *fair, equitable, and professional manner.* 1–2–3
25. Leaders *recognize staff accomplishments.* 1–2–3

## Tabulations

Average Subtotal: 1) Total the scores by category for each questionnaire and 2) average the scores for the group and place in the appropriate category as follows:

- Alignment _____
- Atmosphere/attitude _____
- Accountability _____
- Adept leadership _____

## Level of Connectedness*

Subtotal Average Ranking:

- High level of effectiveness: 64–75 (85th percentile+)
- Moderate level of effectiveness: 56–63 (75th–84th percentile)
- Marginal level of effectiveness: 48–55 (64th–74th percentile)
- Ineffective level: 47 and below (63rd percentile and below)

Item Analysis:

- Each question has a value of (1) low, (2) moderate, (3) high.
- Correlate the total value of the group for each question to the italicized key words (i.e., alignment #1 = "x"); assign an average score per item for each group.

Total Strength of Ranking: Total the average scores for each group by category and apply the following ranking:

- High level of effectiveness: 255–300 (85th percentile+)
- Moderate level of effectiveness: 225–254 (75th–84th percentile)
- Marginal level of effectiveness: 192–224 (64th–73rd percentile)
- Ineffective level: 189 and below (63rd percentile and below)

*The subtotals and totals are guides in determining the level of connectedness or disconnection with a school or school district. It is highly recommended that concerns highlighted by this assessment instrument are verified through group interviews with the school board, administration, teachers, support staff, parents, and students.

# A-2: SCHOOL SYSTEMS "CROSS CHECK": ABBREVIATED (2021)

## Background

The School Systems "Cross Check" attempts to evaluate the overall effectiveness of a school or school district by examining the following four key elements: alignment, atmosphere/attitude or culture, accountability, and adept leadership. Underlying the evaluation of these four elements is an understanding that a school and school district can significantly improve instruction when these four elements are operationally interconnected.

## Directions

Review the key words under each category and place an 'X' next to those that do not represent the school or district's focus in the designated category.

## Alignment

Focus: All practices, processes, and goals are aligned from the "boardroom" to the classroom.

| | |
|---|---|
| __Instructional plan | __Instructional Programs |
| __Annual Review | __Student Achievement |
| __Measurable Goals | __Action Plans |
| __District Goals | __Outcomes/Targets |
| __Values, Vision | __Expectations |
| __Assessments | __Benchmarks |
| __Multiyear Plans | __Decision-making |
| __"Day-to-Day" Work | __Communication |

## Atmosphere/Attitude/Culture

Focus: To build a culture of teamwork, collaboration, and positive attitude that maximizes the talents of employees in creating a high-performing organization.

| | |
|---|---|
| __Values | __"Buy-in" |
| __Professional Development | __Mentoring |
| __Providing Time for Collaboration | __Coaching |

| | |
|---|---|
| __Problem Solving | __Differentiated Development |
| __Empowers Staff | __Providing Adequate Resources |
| __Reinforces Desired Attitude | __"Child First" Mantra |
| __"Right People on the Bus" | __Instructional Focus |
| __Shared Responsibility | __Group Recognition |

## Accountability

Focus: To design a systemic, customized, continuous improvement model with measurable benchmark indicators and processes that monitor and adjust effectiveness.

| | |
|---|---|
| __Targeted Outcomes | __Helpful Observations |
| __Individual Accountability | __Criteria-Based Evaluations |
| __Group Accountability | __Teacher Goals |
| __Motivational Program | __Action Research |
| __Communicated Expectations | __Assists Professional Growth |
| __Data Driven | __Measurement Proficiency |
| __Multiple Sources of Data | __Proficient Data Analysis |
| __Quarterly/Annual Progress Reviews | __Data Linked to Planning |
| __Transparent Reporting | __Indicators of Success |

## Adept Leadership

Focus: To develop a collaborative model that assists in aligning every aspect of the organization to achieve a higher performance level and excellence.

| | |
|---|---|
| __Leads Goal Development | __Inclusive |
| __Long-Short Range Planning | __Risk Taking |
| __Reinforces Values/Beliefs | __Engages Stakeholders |
| __Eliminates Ineffective Programs | __Seeks Resources |
| __Eliminates Distractions | __Reinforces Teamwork |
| __"Laser Focused" | __Values People |
| __Influences Progress | __Encourages Growth |
| __Flexible | __Problem Solver |
| __Effective Communicator | __Models Values, Beliefs |
| __Organized Frameworks and Structures | __Assumes Responsibility |
| __Demonstrates Expertise | __Stakeholder Engagement |
| __Fosters an Environment for Success | __Fair and Equitable |
| __Provides for Recognition | |

*All data requires verification through a group interview process (i.e., department, grade level, etc.)

## A-3: DOCUMENT REVIEW AND ANALYSIS

This instrument provides a rubric to review and analyze documents, as well as school/district policies and practices. While this instrument can be used as a stand-alone assessment, it is designed to further support the data acquired from conducting the School Systems "Cross Check."

Documents for potential review involved the following organizational areas:

- Strategic plans/school and district goals
- Human resources recruitment and hiring
- Curriculum and programming
- Instructional practices and methodology
- System of assessment and achievement data
- Observation/supervision and evaluation practices
- Professional development
- Financial planning: Priorities and allocations
- Communication
- Board policies

*A rubric is used to rate the quality of the document, policy, or practices in the context of how each contributes to student achievement and higher performance.

**The rubric has defined criteria that correlates to high performing schools and districts. The ratings are as follows:

- 3: Correlates to *higher* outcomes and instructional quality
- 2: *Moderate* correlation to higher outcomes
- 1: *Low* correlation

***Interviews with appropriate leadership team members are recommended to validate conclusions or generalizations associated with the rating.

### Document Review Rubric

*Ratings/Criteria*

Directions: Rate the designated areas based on the following rubric values/descriptions. Check all that apply.

## 3

Documents and plans *reflect* current district strategic planning and thinking.
Organizational documents *align* with organizational outcomes.
Processes and Practices are *consistent* with targeted goals and outcomes.
The mission, vision, values, and beliefs are *embedded*.
Best practices are *represented* in the documents, policies, and practices.
Policies and practices *contribute* to an environment of "continuous improvement."
An optimum learning environment is a *result* of quality practices and policies.
Policies *contribute* to organizational effectiveness.
Policies, practices, and documents *contribute* to a professional environment.

## 2

Documents and plans are *inconsistent* in reflecting current district planning and thinking.
Organizational documents *sporadically* align with organizational outcomes.
Processes and practices are *inconsistent* with targeted goals and outcomes.
The mission, vision, values, and beliefs are *periodically* mentioned in documents.
Best practices are *somewhat represented* in the documents, practices, and policies.
The documents, practices, and policies *may contribute* to "continuous improvement."
The learning environment is *less than ideal*.
Policies contributing to organizational effectiveness are *not consistent* in all areas.
The professional environment is *hindered* by the district's practices and policies.

## 1

Documents and planning *do not reflect* current district strategic planning and thinking.
Organizational documents *do not align* with organizational outcomes.
Processes and practices *do not target* desired goals and outcomes.

Mission, vision, values, and beliefs statements are *not represented* in documents.

There is *no evidence* of best practices in documents, practices, and policies.

An environment of "continuous improvement" is *nonexistent*.

The learning environment is *poor*.

Policies *do not contribute* to organizational effectiveness.

A professional environment is *non-existent*.

### Document/Practice/Policy Summary

Strategic plans/school and district goals 1–2–3
Human resources recruitment and hiring 1–2–3
Curriculum and programming 1–2–3
Instructional practices and methodology 1–2–3
System of assessment and achievement data 1–2–3
Observation/supervision and evaluation practices 1–2–3
Professional development 1–2–3
Financial: Budget review/planning/priorities/allocations 1–2–3
Communication 1–2–3
Board policies 1–2–3

Notations:
Average Score*:

*The score represents a guide to identifying the level of effectiveness in how policies and practices complement the process of improving student achievement.

## A-4: HIERARCHY OF SCHOOL/DISTRICT DEVELOPMENT (REVISED EDITION 2021)

Focus: This informal instrument generates discussion among stakeholders regarding the current status of a school or district's achievement level.

Directions: Place a "check" next to the statements in each category if your school or district meets or exceeds the criteria listed.

# Categorization of Development Levels

## World Class****

- Achievement results correlate favorably to exemplary levels of performance on the "Program for International Student Assessment" (PISA) or Trends in International Mathematics and Science Study (TIMSS).
- Student issues/needs, instruction, and learning are a priority.
- High degree of professional creativity and collaboration.
- Individualization and student learning plans are the norm.
- Ranked in the top 5 schools or school districts in the state by the Department of Education or such surveys as *Forbes* and *U.S. News and World Report*.

****Meets criteria in *all* statements listed here; if criteria are not met, proceed to the next category for review.

## Exemplary***

- School and/or school district scores at the highest levels on all state and national assessments (90th percentile on standardized assessments, National Assessments of Educational Progress [NAEP], Scholastic Aptitude Testing [SAT], and Advanced Placement Tests [AP]).
- Executes a strategic instructional plan that focuses on student achievement annually.
- High degree of confidence permeates throughout the organization for its ability to improve instruction and student performance.
- School or district is respected regionally for its instructional program.
- There is evidence of instructional relationships between grades and organizational levels (elementary, middle, and high school).
- Staff retention is high, and applicants are abundant for *all* positions.

***Meets 5 out of 6 criteria listed here; if criteria are not met, proceed to the next category for review.

## Advancing**

- School and/or district has demonstrated continuous and steady growth on state and national assessments.

- On an annual basis, the school or district moves students from underperformance to proficiency but still has a significant number of students scoring in the non-proficient range.
- Seeks solutions and refines initiatives to improve its achievement deficiencies.
- Builds the school or district's internal professional capacity in addressing achievement issues.
- Sorting out challenges related to instructional time and collaboration between departments and grade levels.
- Competitive in the recruitment process.

**Meets 5 out of 6 criteria listed here; if criteria are not met, proceed to the next category for review.

## Maintenance*

- School or district performance remains stagnant during a period of several years or student proficiency consistency falls below acceptable "cutoffs" for performance at the state level.
- Little focus on instructional improvement.
- Strong deference to "tradition" and past practices regardless of success or failure of these practices or programs.
- District or school struggles to fill positions.
- Survival issues related to funding, safety, discipline, retention, and enrollment dominate the conversation.
- Goal attainment is sporadic or inconsistent at best.

*Meets any one or more of the criteria in this category.

Notation: It should be recognized that the categories and placement in any given category are subjective. The instrument is designed to evoke discussion regarding a school or district's current level of functioning and ascertain its aspirational level for improvement.

# Appendix B
## *Leadership Training Module*

These slides can be converted to PowerPoint with permission. The slides are provided for school leaders to utilize in sensitizing and training team members for leadership roles in improving student achievement and school performance. Designed to stimulate discussion, leaders are afforded the opportunity to reflect on a school or district's status in improving instruction and creating schools with a focus on higher performance.

### SLIDE #1: TITLE PAGE

"Leadership and Excellence"

### SLIDE #2: INTRODUCTION—YODA QUOTE

"Try Not."

"Do or Do Not."

"There is no try."

### SLIDE #3: REFLECTIVE QUESTIONS

**Crisis in Education?**

- Inability to move "achievement"? Why?
- Current focus: Socioeconomic, mental health, etc.?
- Stakeholder paralysis
- Lack of "will"
- Worth the investment?

### SLIDE #4: SIMPLE QUESTIONS

What kind of schools do you want for children?

Are you willing to make a commitment to high performing schools?

How might that be accomplished?

**Different Stakeholder Answers for each question?**

- Board
- Superintendent
- Teachers
- Parents
- Community

### SLIDE #5: QUESTION

What does "ALL" really mean?

- Mediocrity?
- "Teaching to the Middle"
- "Lower Standards

Or

"Raising the Bar for Everyone"

### SLIDE #6

Student Achievement

Continuum of Improvement

*Appendix B*

Stagnant

Progressing

Declining

**SLIDE #7**

Mirror Test

**How do you define your school or district?**

- Not going anywhere.
- Keeping the "lid" on issues?
- "Status quo"?
- Continuously improving?
- "Knocking it out of the park?"
- "Always moving toward the Horizon!"

**SLIDE #8**

More Questions

Is "good" "good enough"?

or

Is just "okay" "okay"?

**SLIDE #9**

Familiar Statements

**What is the real meaning behind them?**

- "We do a great job."
- "We are a great school."

- "We make the most of what we have."
- "Parents and students love it here."

## SLIDE #10

The Deep Five Dive

Good Schools*

Relevance

Rigor

Engagement

Inclusion (ALL)

Competitive

*regionally, state, nationally, globally

## SLIDE #11

Assessments/Growth in Achievement

National Assessment of Educational Progress

### Reading

- Average reading score of 4th grade students in 2017 not significantly different compared to 2015
- Lower-performing 4th grade students scored lower in reading in 2017 than compared to 2015

### Mathematics

- No significant change in average mathematics score for 4th graders compared to 2015

- Decrease in mathematics score for lower-performing 4th grade students compared to 2015

## SLIDE #12

International Comparisons

Program for International Student Assessment

PISA 2015

- Mathematics: 35th
- Reading: 16th
- Science: 20th

**Comparison 2012 to 2015**

- The United States saw an 11-point drop in average score for math.
- U.S. reading and science scores were relatively flat.

## SLIDE #13

**Discussion**

Is it fair to compare the United States to other countries?

Are we different?

Excuse or Clarification?

## SLIDE #14

Investment/Initiatives versus Results

Governmental: Federal, State, Local

Initiatives/Reforms

Revenue and Investment

Legislation/Mandates

## SLIDE #15

Lack of Academic Competitiveness

**Significance**

- Lack of student growth
- Declining economic growth
- Loss of intellectual advantage
- General instability

## SLIDE #16

**Reflective Question**

Have you ever asked yourself, despite programs, initiatives, and reforms designed to address lagging student achievement, why is my school or district not meeting or exceeding expectations?

## SLIDE #17

Why: Lack of Progress

Common Explanations

**Socioeconomic**

- Poverty
- Family structure
- Importance/value of education

*Appendix B*

### Funding

- Lack of investment: State, school board, facilities

### Internal Capacity

- Professional Development

### Governmental Interference

Federal and State Mandates (Curriculum, Assessments, etc.)

**SLIDE #18**

Excuses

or

Benign Neglect

### Reinforces

- Low expectations
- Limited aspirations
- Poor performance

**SLIDE #19**

Why: No Progress

"Under-the-Radar" Explanations

### Disconnections

- Alignment, attitude, accountability, and adept leadership
- Perceptions: Board, administration, teachers, parents, community

## Implementation Issues

- Process
- Procedures

## Stakeholder Paralysis

- Failure to commit
- Inability to develop consensus

## SLIDE #20

## Significant Challenges

- Global competition
- Technology revolution
- Building high-performing schools
- Equity and excellence
- All students
- All schools
- Performance outcomes

## SLIDE #21

Common Solutions

(Ineffective)

Program Layering

"Silver Bullets"

Legislative Mandates

School Business Models

## Old-School Remedies

Back in the day: "When I went to school, I walked up hill to school both ways."

*Appendix B*

## SLIDE #22

Real Impediments

**Leadership Issues**

- Lack of focus: Goals, plans, outcomes
- Flawed planning, implementation, and execution
- Supervision, evaluation, and monitoring

**Process Issues**

- Formulaic solutions
- Design and planning
- Consensus building
- Empowerment

**Instructional/Curriculum/Delivery Issues**

## SLIDE #23

**Reflective Question**

Have you ever wondered how, despite the odds, some schools and districts are able to succeed?

and

What will it take for my school to become high performing?

## SLIDE #24

High-Performance Criteria

Interdisciplinary

Technological

Research and Relevance

Critical Inferential Assignments

Experimentation

Project-Based Learning

Focus on Writing and Research

Results/Outcomes Orientations

## SLIDE #25

How Can a School or District Become High-Achieving?

Customized Plan

Identify the Disconnections

Research-Based and Proven Solutions

Internal versus External Solutions

Collaborative, Shared Leadership

Build External Capacity

Understanding the Interrelationship of Key Elements

## SLIDE #26

**Reflective Question**

What type of school or district do you believe that you are?

World Class

Exemplary

Advancing

Maintenance

What type of school do you want to be?


**SLIDE # 27**

Hierarchy of School/District Development Instrument

Informal

and

Self-Reflection

Know where you are!

and

Know where you want to be!

# Appendix C
## *Leadership Skills That Ignite Performance*

School improvement necessitates that leaders have a skill set to facilitate change. The transformation process of moving a school or district to one that is higher performing requires a foundational understanding of the key elements that drive improvement. Leaders also must be skillful in maneuvering the improvement process through a myriad of obstacles.

This section provides a series of slides that can be used to orient leadership teams with skills and background information prior to implementation. These slides can be converted into a PowerPoint presentation with permission.

### SLIDE #1

Leadership Defines

- Commitment
- Parameters
- Managerial style
- Exerts influence

### SLIDE #2

The Commitment to Performance

Breaking Down Paradoxical Barriers

- Identify stakeholders
- Understand the factors impeding full commitment
- Define the process
- Leadership
- Courage

## SLIDE #3

Parameters to Performance

- "Child-first" focus
- Systemic
- Analytical
- Instructional
- Measurable

## SLIDE #4

Performance Leadership Skills

Synergistic

Strategic

"Synertegic"

## SLIDE #5

Situational Leadership

Wizard or Warrior?

*Appendix C* 113

## SLIDE #6

**Building a Performance Team**

Recruitment and Hiring Process

Strategic Selection of Personnel

Attributes for Success

Attitude

Character

Verifiable/Comparable Skills

Platform for Success

Organizational Chemistry

## SLIDE #7

"Performance is Key"

but

"If you don't know where you are going, you might not get there."—Yogi Berra

## SLIDE #8

Visualize

Imagine!

Believe!

Plan!

Act!

## SLIDE #9

The Essential Elements

Alignment

Atmosphere/Attitude/Culture

Accountability

Adept Leadership

## SLIDE #10

Correlation to Interconnectivity of Elements

Higher Degree of Connectivity = Higher Level of Performance

Lower Degree of Connectivity = Increased # Disconnections

## SLIDE #11

Variables to Achievement/Student Growth

Questions?????

*What can a school or district control?*

*What is beyond a school or district's control?*

## SLIDE #12

Focus on Achievement Policies and Practices

*Core Beliefs*

All children learn!

Students always come first!

Failure is *not* an option!

Atmosphere/Culture of Continuous Improvement!

Nothing can take the place of good, quality instruction!

Invest in the internal capacity of the organization!

# Bibliography

Anthony, Scott, and Evan I. Schwartz. "What the Best Transformation Leaders Do," *Harvard Business Review*, May 8, 2017, p. 2. https://hbr.org/2017/05.

Avossa, Robert. "Looking to June: Top Five Learning Priorities," *Learning Counsel*, 2020, p. 1. https://www.thelearningcounsel.com/article/looking-to-june-top-five-learning-priorities.

Best, Jane, and Allison Dunlap. "Continuous Improvement in Schools and Districts: Policy Considerations," McRel International, October 2020, p. 1. https://files.eric.gov/fulltext/ ED557599.pdf.

Blank, Rolf, Doreen Langesen, and Adam Peterman. "State Indicators of Science and Mathematics Education 2007," *Counsel of Chief State School Officers*, 2007, p. 3–4.

Blume, Howard. "LAUSD Students Suffered Alarming Harm during Pandemic," *Los Angeles Times*, March 31, 2021. https://www.latimes.com/california/story/2021-03-31/lausd-covid-data-show-alarming-learning-harm-report.

Boston Public Schools. "Boston Students Again Outperform Urban Peers on Nation's Report Card." https://www.bostonpublicschools.org/site/default.aspx?PageTyp...=047e6be3-6d87-4130-8424-d8e49ed6c2a&FlexDataID=3158.

Boston Public Schools. "Update on Eliminating the Achievement Gap," Presentation to School Committee, June 18, 2014, p. 3. https://www.bostonpublicschools.org/cms/lib07.

Boston Public Schools. "Whole Improvement: Six Essentials." Internet Archive, 2009. https://archive.org/ details/publicscho04.

Bryant, Adam. "Leadership: Building the Skillset," *New York Times*, 2020, p. 8.

CASEL. "What Is Social and Emotional Learning?" https://casel.org/what-is-sel/.

CBS News. "How to Lead: Wisdom from the World's Greatest CEO's, Founders, and Game Changers," John Dickerson interviewing David Rubenstein, cofounder and coexecutive chairman of the Carlyle Group on *Face the Nation*, filmed September 6, 2020. https://cbsnews.com/news/fulltranscript-of-face-thenation-september-6-2020/.

Clark, Geoffrey. "Watch: Jim Valvano Gives Memorable 1993 ESPYs Speech," *USA Today*, December 8, 2020. https://www.fightingirishwire.usatoday2020/12/08.

CNN. "Last Look: Schools in the Age of COVID-19," Freed Zakaria, GPS, filmed April 4, 2021. https://cnn.com/videos/tv/2021/04/exp-gps-0404-last-look-on-schools.cnn

Committee for Children 2012–2021. "Moving from All Students to Each Student," *Second Step*. https://secondstep.org/success-stories/everett.

Cortright, Bradley. "Bloomberg Says Teachers Are 'Just Going to Have to Suck It Up' and Have in-Person Classes Amid Pandemic," *Independent Journal Review*, February 3, 2021, https://ijr.com/bloomberg-teachers-suck-it-up-have-in-person-classes/.

Cotter, Vincent F. *Igniting School Performance: A Pathway from Academic Paralysis to Excellence*. Lanham, MD: Rowman & Littlefield, 2019.

Cotter, Vincent F., and Robert D. Hassler. *Performance Is Key: Connecting the Links to Leadership and Excellence*. Lanham, MD: Rowman & Littlefield, 2018.

Darwin, Charles. *On the Origin of Species: By Means of Natural Selection—the Preservation of Favoured Races in the Struggle for Life*. London: John Murray, 1859.

Economy, Peter. "These 14 Amazon Leadership Practices Can Lead You and Your Business to Remarkable Success," *Inc.*, November 8, 2019. https://www.inc.com/peter-economy/the-14-amazon-leadership-principles-that-can-lead-you-your-business-to-tremendous-success.html.

Evers, Tony, and Chris Minnich. *School and District FAQs—Identification of Schools*. Washington, DC: Council of Chief State Officers, 2016.

Gerwertz, Catherine. "Instruction during COVID-19: Less Learning Time Drives Fears of Academic Erosion," *Education Week*, May 28, 2020. https://www.edweek.org/ew/articles/2020/05/27/instruction-during-covid-19-less-learning-time-drives.html.

Gladwell, Malcolm. *The Tipping Point: How Little Things Can Make a Big Difference*. New York: Little, Brown, 2000.

Goldstein, Dana. "Research Shows Students Falling Months Behind during Virus," *New York Times*, June 5, 2020. https://www.nytimes.com/2020/06/05/us/coronavirus-education-lost-learning.html.

Hanna, Maddle, Kristen A. Graham, and Melanie Berney. "COVID-19 Has Upended Education. How Will Schools Solve the Learning Loss?" *Philadelphia Inquirer*, August 8, 2021. https://www.inquirer.com/education/a/pennsylvania-education-students-pandemic-learning-loss-20210408.html

Hartford Public Schools. "District Model for Excellence—Strategic Plan 2018–2022." https://hartfordschools.org/districtmodel/.

Hill, Heather C., and Susanna Loeb. "Teachers Will Need to Work Together to Uncover Missed Learning," *Education Week*, May 27, 2020. https://www.edweek.org/ew/articles/2020/05/28.

Honig, Meredith, Michael Copeland, Lydia Rainey, and Morena Newton. *Central Office Transformation for District-Wide Teaching and Learning Improvement*. Commissioned by the Wallace foundation for the Study of Teaching and Policy. Seattle: University of Washington, 2010.

Hunt, Ben. "You Are What Your Record Says You Are," *Epsilon Theory*, November 3, 2018, p. 2. https://www.epsilontheory.com/you-are-what-your-record-says-you-are/.

Izumi, Lance T. *What Works: Inside Model Charter Schools*. Lincoln, IL: Center on Innovation and Improvement, Academic Development Institute, 2008.

John F. Kennedy Quotations. *Economics, Public Papers of Presidents: John F. Kennedy, 1962*. Remarks in Pueblo, Colorado, following the Approval of the Frying-Pan Arkansas Project (336), August 17, 1962, John F. Kennedy Presidential Library and Museum.

Kamenetz, Anya. "Keep Schools Open All Summer, and Other Bold Ideas to Help Kids Catch Up," *NPR Education*, February 8, 2021, p. 2–5.

Kane, Thomas, Antoniya M. Owens, William H. Marinell, Daniel R. C. Thal, and Douglas O. Staiger. *Teaching Higher: Educators' Perspective on Common Core Implementation*. Cambridge, MA: Harvard University Center for Policy Research, 2016. https://cepr.harvard.edu/files/teaching-higher-report.pdf.

KIPP: NYC Public Schools. "Our Core Values." https://www.kippnyc.org/kipps-core-values/.

Kozol, Jonathan. *Savage Inequities*. New York: Harper Perennial, 1991.

Lee, Victoria, Emily Gutierrez, and Kristin Blagg. "Declining School Enrollment Spells Trouble for Education Funding," *Urban Wire*, October 6, 2020. https://www.urban.org/urban-wire/declining-school-enrollment-spells-trouble-education-funding.

Lezotte, Lawrence W. *Sustainable School Reform: The District Context for School Improvement*. Okemos, MI: Effective Schools Products, 1991.

Lieberman, Mark. "Top U.S. Companies: These are the Skills Students Need in a Post-Pandemic World," *Education Week*, March 2, 2021. https://www.edweek.org/technology/top-u-s-companies-these-are-the-skills-students-need-in-a-post-pandemic-world.

Lynch, Matthew. "Becoming a Transformational School," *Edvocate*, January 6, 2015. https://www.theedvocate.org/becoming-a-transformational-schoo-leader.

Master Schools. "Welcome to Mastery Schools." https://masterycharter.org.

Middle States Commission on Elementary and Secondary Schools. *Excellence by Design: Queen Anne's County Public Schools Self-Study Report: The Plan for Growth and Improvement*. Philadelphia, PA: Middle States Commission on Elementary and Secondary Schools, February 10, 2010.

Natanson, Hannah. "Failing Grade Spike in Virginia's Largest School System as Online Learning Gap Emerges Nationwide," *Washington Post*, November 24, 2020. https://www.washingtonpost.com/local/education/fairfax-schools-more-failing-grades/2020/11/24/1ac2412e-2e34-11eb-96c2-aac3f162215d_story.html.

National Assessment of Educational Progress. "National Assessment of Educational Progress Nations Report Card, 2019." *National Assessment of Educational Progress*, 2019. https://nces.ed.gov/nationsreportcard/subject/publications/stt2019/pdf/2020014NP4.pdf.

National Charter School Resource Center. "Frequently Asked Questions," *National Charter School Resource Center*, September 13, 2018. http://52.61.52.139/faqs.

National Commission on Excellence. *A Nation at Risk: The Imperative for Educational Reform.* Washington, DC: Government Printing Office, 1983. https://files.eric.ed.gov/fulltext/.

Neill, A. S. *Freedom Not License.* New York: Hart, 1966.

Oregon Department of Education. "Continuous Improvement Process and Planning," *Oregon Department of Education*, March 25, 2021. https://www.oregon.gov/ode/schools-and-districts.

Park, S., S. Hironaka, P. Carver, and L. Nordstrum. "Continuous Improvement in Education," *Carnegie Foundation or the Advancement of Teaching*, 2013. https://carnegiefoundation.org/sites/default/files/Carnegie-foundation_continuous-improvement-2013.05.pdf.

Partelow, Lisette, and Sarah Shapiro. "Curriculum Reform in the Nation's Largest School Districts," *Center for American Progress*, August 28, 2018. https://americanprogress.org/issues/education-K-12-reports/2018/08/29/454704.

Pasadena Independent School District, "Strategic Plan 2020–2025." https://pasadenaisd.org.

Pennsylvania Department of Education. "Act 18 of 2019 (SB 144)," *Pennsylvania Department of Education*, June 28, 2019. https://www.education.pa.gov/Schools/safeschools/laws/Pages/Act44.aspx?text=Act%2018%2020%20revi.

Przybyla, Heidi. "Federal Officials Seek Better Rules about Schools' Indoor Air Quality," NBC News, May 20, 2021. https://apples.news/A2-CTgeULSpu9xRnLBNE0KW.

Q.E.D. Foundation. "Transformational Change Model," *Q.E.D. Foundation*, June 2012. https://www.qedfoundation.org/transformational-change-model-2/.

Reh, John F. "Pareto Principle or the 80/20 Rule," *Balance Careers*, October 23, 2019. https://thebalancecareers.com/pareto-s-principle-the-80-20-rule-2275148.

Research for Better Teaching. "Empowering Sustainable School Improvement—Our Approach," *Research for Better Teaching*, 2016. https://www.rbteach.com/why-rbt/ourapproach.

Rice, Tim, and Andrew Lloyd Webber. "Jesus Christ Superstar, What's the Buzz Lyrics." *Metro Lyrics.* https://www.metrolyrics.com/what-the-buzz-jesus-christ-superstar.html.

Richards, Erin. "Math Scores Stink in America: Other Countries Teach It Differently and See Higher Achievement," *USA Today*, February 28, 2020. https://www.usatoday.com/story/news/education/2020.

Ricks, Thomas E. *First Principles.* New York: HarperCollins, 2020.

Robert Greenleaf Center for Servant Leadership. "Start Here: What Is Servant Leadership?" *Robert Greenleaf Center for Servant Leadership*, April 17, 2021. https://www.greenleafcenter.org/what-is-servant-leadership/.

Room, Tony. "It Shouldn't Take a Pandemic: Coronavirus Exposed Internet Inequality among U.S. Students as Schools Close Their Doors," *Washington Post*, March 16, 2020. https://www.washingtonpost.com/technology/2020/03/16/schools-internet-inequality-coronavirus/.

Schroeder, Laurie Mason. "Another School Closed for Mold," *Allentown Morning Call*, September 9, 2018. https://mcall.com/news/breaking.

Scorese, Martin. dir., *Goodfellas.* Los Angeles: Warner Brothers, 1990.

Second Step. "Success Stories Everett." https://www.secondstep.org/success-stories/everett.

Sparks, Sarah D. "Growth Mindset Linked to Higher Test Scores, Students Well-Being in Global Study," *Education Week*, April 21, 2021. https://www.edweek.org/leadership/growth-mindset-linked-to-higher-test-scores-student-well-being-in-global-study/2021/04.

Steiner, David. *Curriculum Research: What We Know and Where We Need to Go*. Washington, DC: Standard Work, 2017. https://standardwork.org/wp-content/uploads/2017/03/sw-curriculum-research-report-fnl.pdf.

Stuart, Elizabeth, and Leah Asmelash. "A Rise in Student Suicides Has Pushed the 5th Largest School District to Speed Up a Return to in-Person Learning," *CNN*, January 26, 2021. https://www.cnn.com/us/clark-county-school-district-covid-suicide-trnd/index.html.

Tillson, Tom. "Report: Baltimore H.S. Senior Passes Just 3 Classes in 4 Years, Still Near Top of His Class," *BPR: Business and Politics*, March 5, 2021. https://www.bizacreview.com/2021/03/05/report-baltimore-hs-senior-passes-just-3-classes-in-4yrs-still-near-top-of-his-class.

U.S. Department of Education. "No Child Left Behind" Public Law 107-110, Elementary and Secondary Education Act 2001." https://www2.ed.gov/nclb/landing.jhtml.

U.S. Department of Education. "Race to the Top: Game-Changing Reforms, ED Recovery Act: American Recovery and Reinvestment Act of 2009." https://www.ed.gov/open/plan/race-to-top-game-changing-reforms.

U.S. Department of Education. "Race to the Top Executive Summary, ED Recovery Act: American Recovery and Reinvestment Act of 2009." https://www.nes.ed.gov/.

Webster, Merriam. "Definition of Gestalt." https://www.meriam-webster.com/dictionary/gestalt.

Zakrzewski, Vicki. "A New Model of School Reform," *Greater Good Science Center-Berkeley*, May 21, 2014. https://greatgoodberkely.edu/article/item/a-model-of-school-reform.

# About the Author

**Vincent F. Cotter**, as superintendent of schools, was the primary innovator of a unique school improvement program that dramatically improved student achievement. For his efforts, he was awarded the prestigious American Society for Quality's International Juran Medal (2011) in the field of education for sustained systemic improvement. Cotter cofounded the Exemplary Schools Organization to improve the academic performance of schools and school districts.

www.ingramcontent.com/pod-product-compliance
Lightning Source LLC
Chambersburg PA
CBHW030143240426
43672CB00005B/247